I0483864

Franchise Business:
A Powerful Winning Strategy for Business Growth in Any Economy

By Ade Asefeso MCIPS MBA

First Edition

ISBN-13: 978-1511652988

ISBN-10: 1511652985

Publisher: AA Global Sourcing Ltd
Website: http://www.aaglobalsourcing.com

Table of Contents

Disclaimer

This publication is designed to provide competent and reliable information regarding the subject matter covered. However, it is sold with the understanding that the author and publisher are not engaged in rendering professional advice. The authors and publishers specifically disclaim any liability that is incurred from the use or application of contents of this book.

If you purchased this book without a cover you should be aware that this book may have been stolen property and reported as "unsold and destroyed" to the publisher. In this case neither the author nor the publisher has received any payment for this "stripped book."

Dedication

To my family and friends who seems to have been sent here to teach me something about who I am supposed to be. They have nurtured me, challenged me, and even opposed me.... But at every juncture has taught me!

This book is dedicated to my lovely boys, Thomas, Michael and Karl. Teaching them to manage their finance will give them the lives they deserve. They have taught me more about life, presence, and energy management than anything I have done in my life.

Chapter 1: Introduction

Franchising is a continuing relationship in which a franchisor provides a licensed privilege to the franchisee to do business and offers assistance in organizing, training, merchandising, marketing and managing in return for a monetary consideration. Franchising is a form of business by which the owner (franchisor) of a product, service or method obtains distribution through affiliated dealers (franchisees).

Franchising is one of three business strategies a company may use in capturing market share. The others are company owned units or a combination of company owned and franchised units.

Franchising is a business strategy for getting and keeping customers. It is a marketing system for creating an image in the minds of current and future customers about how the company's products and services can help them. It is a method for distributing products and services that satisfy customer needs.

Franchising is a network of interdependent business relationships that allows a number of people to share:
1. A brand identification.
2. A successful method of doing business.
3. A proven marketing and distribution system.

In short, franchising is a strategic alliance between groups of people who have specific relationships and responsibilities with a common goal to dominate markets, i.e., to get and keep more customers than their competitors.

There are many misconceptions about franchising, but probably the most widely held is that you as a franchisee are "buying a franchise." In reality you are investing your assets in a system to utilize the brand name, operating system and ongoing support. You and everyone in the system are licensed to use the brand name and operating system.

The business relationship is a joint commitment by all franchisees to get and keep customers. Legally you are bound to get and keep them using the prescribed marketing and operating systems of the franchisor.

To be successful in franchising you must understand the business and legal ramifications of your relationship with the franchisor and all the franchisees. Your focus must be on working with other franchisees and company managers to market the brand, and fully use the operating system to get and keep customers.

Other franchisees and company operated units are not your competition. The opposite is true. They and you share the task of establishing the brand as the dominant brand in all markets entered and reinforcing the customer's familiarity with and trust in the brand. So in this respect you are working as a team with others in the system. Other franchisees share with you the responsibility for quality, consistency, convenience, and other factors that define your franchise and insures repeat business for everyone.

Increasing the value of the brand name is a shared responsibility of the franchisor and franchisee.

An "ownership mentality" destroys the reason franchised and company-operated units are successful. Think about it. If you think you "bought" a franchise, you become an "owner" and begin to think and act like an owner. You will want to change the system because of your needs, you will wonder what you are paying the royalty for, and you will begin thinking of other franchisees as your competitors. For these and many other reasons you do not want to think of yourself as an "independent owner."

As a franchisee you own the assets of your company, which you have chosen to invest in someone else's brand and operating system and ongoing support. You own the assets of your company, but you are licensed to operate someone else's business system.

Your desire to become a franchisee must be grounded in your belief that you can be more successful using someone else's brand and operating according to their systems and methods, than you could if you opened up your own independent business and competed against them. You want to look for a franchisor who is building a system of interdependent franchisees who are committed to getting and keeping customers, to growing faster than the market, to growing faster than the competitors, and to do all of that with high margins. When you discover a franchisor who understands this relationship, you have a franchisor worth your consideration.

If buying an existing business doesn't sound right for you but starting from scratch sounds a bit intimidating, you could be suited for franchise ownership. Just what is a franchise and how do you know if you're cut out to be a franchisee? Essentially, a franchisee pays an initial fee and ongoing royalties to a franchisor; in return, the franchisee gains the use of a trademark, ongoing support from the franchisor, and the right to use the franchisor's system of doing business and sell its products or services.

In addition to a well-known brand name, buying a franchise offers many other advantages that are not available to the entrepreneur starting a business from scratch. Perhaps the most significant is that you get a proven system of operation and training in how to use it. New franchisees can avoid a lot of the mistakes start-up entrepreneurs typically make because the franchisor has already perfected daily operations through trial and error.

Reputable franchisors conduct market research before selling a new outlet, so you will feel greater confidence that there is a demand for the product or service. The franchisor also provides you a clear picture of the competition and how to differentiate yourself from them.

Franchisees enjoy the benefit of strength in numbers. You will gain from economics of scale in buying materials, supplies and services, such as advertising, as well as in negotiating for locations and lease terms. By comparison, independent operators have to negotiate on their own, usually getting less favourable terms.

Some suppliers won't deal with new businesses or will reject your business because your account isn't big enough.

Once you have decided a franchise is the right route for you, how do you choose the right one? With so many franchise systems to choose from, the options can be dizzying. Start by investigating various industries that interest you to find those with growth potential. Narrow the choices to a few industries you are most interested in, then analyze your geographic area to see if there is a market for that type of business. If so, contact all the franchise companies in those fields and ask them for information on their franchise opportunity. Any reputable company will be happy to send you information at no cost.

Of course, you shouldn't rely solely on these promotional materials to make your decision. You also need to do your own detective work. Start by visiting your library or going online to look up all the magazine and newspaper articles you can find about the company you are considering. Is the company depicted favourably? Does it seem to be well managed and growing?

Once you have decided on a certain franchise through your preliminary research, you need to find out if this opportunity is as good as it sounds. Your next step is to analyze it thoroughly to determine whether it's really worth buying.

Much of the information you will need to gather in order to analyze a franchise will be acquired through the following:
1. Interviews with the franchisor.
2. Interviews with existing franchisees.
3. Examination of the franchise.
4. Uniform Franchise Offering Circular (UFOC).
5. Examination of the franchise agreement.
6. Examination of the franchise's audited financial statements.
7. An earnings-claim statement or sample unit income (profit-and-loss) statement.
8. Trade-area surveys.
9. List of current franchisees.
10. Newspaper or magazine articles about the franchise.
11. A list of the franchisor's current assets and liabilities.

Through this research, you want to find out the following:
1. If the franchisor as well as the current franchisees are profitable.
2. How well-organized the franchise is.
3. If it has national adaptability.
4. Whether it has good public acceptance.
5. What its unique selling proposition is.
6. How good the financial controls of the business are.
7. If the franchise is credible.
8. What kind of exposure the franchise has received and the public's reaction to it.
9. If the cash requirements are reasonable.

10. What the integrity and commitment of the franchisor are.
11. If the franchisor has a monitoring system.
12. Which goods are proprietary and must be purchased from the franchisor.
13. What the success ratio is in the industry.

Don't be shy about asking for the required materials from the franchisor. After all, they will be checking you out just as completely. If they aren't, that should sound a warning bell. Another warning sign is if the franchisor asks you to sign a disclaimer stating you haven't relied on any representations not contained in the written agreement. Such a requirement could indicate the franchisor doesn't want to be held responsible for claims made by its sales representatives.

Chapter 2: Why Franchise?

Have a better mousetrap but scared to death that the world is actually beating a path to your door? Trouble sleeping at night wondering who will knock off your operation first? Certain that yours is the next, if only you could get the capital? Tired of reading about companies and thinking, I have a better franchise concept than that company?

Maybe you, too, should consider franchising.

In general, companies decide to begin franchising for one of three reasons; lack of money, people or time.

The primary barrier to expansion that today's entrepreneur faces is lack of capital and franchising allows companies to expand without the risk of debt or the cost of equity. Since franchisees provide the initial investment at the unit level, franchising allows for expansion with minimal capital investment on the part of the franchisor. In addition, since it's the franchisee, and not the franchisor, who signs the lease and commits to various service contracts, franchising allows for expansion with virtually no contingent liability, thus greatly reducing a franchisor's risk.

The second barrier to expansion is finding and retaining good unit managers. All too often, a business owner spends months looking for and training a new manager only to see that manager leave-or worse yet, get hired away by a competitor.

Franchising allows entrepreneurs to overcome many of these problems by substituting a motivated franchisee for a unit manager. Interestingly enough, since the franchisee has both an investment in the unit and a stake in the profits, unit performance will often improve and since a franchisor's income is based on the franchisee's gross sales and not profitability monitoring unit level expenses becomes significantly less cumbersome.

Finally, opening another location takes time. Hunt for sites. Negotiate leases. Arrange for design and build-out. Secure financing. Hire and train staff. Purchase equipment and inventory. The end result is that the number of units you can open in any given period of time is limited by the amount of time it takes to do it properly.

For companies with too little time (or too little staff), franchising is often the fastest way to grow. That is because it's the franchisee who performs most of these growth tasks. The franchisor provides the guidance, of course, but the franchisee does the legwork. Thus franchising not only allows the franchisor financial leverage, but it allows him to leverage his resources as well.

Chapter 3: The 3 Ways a Franchise Business is Organized

A franchise offers a good business opportunity to aspiring entrepreneurs because it is a familiar name customers recognize. Furthermore, the franchise parent company takes the responsibility for training the franchise owner in getting the business off the ground. Franchise contracts tend to be fairly specific in what franchise owners should and should not do, except when it comes to choosing the business structure. Refer to your franchise agreement to ensure your compliance with the agreement, as it might list the business structure options.

1. Sole Proprietorship

A sole proprietorship is considered the easiest type of business structure to organize and register. The sole proprietor registers the business in his name alone, thus giving the business owner the right to all assets but also making the business owner entirely responsible for all debts and financial liabilities. The sole proprietorship is considered the least expensive type of business organization to register, thus making it the most popular business structure among small business owners. At the same time, the sole proprietor should bear in mind that if the franchise fails, he can become personally responsible for the debts. In the event that the franchise location cannot sustain itself, the owner is liable to pay off all debts that the individual location has accrued, and the owner's personal assets are not protected.

2. Limited Liability Company (LLC)

A limited liability company, or an LLC, limits the personal liability of the owner; known as a "member" within the LLC structure and makes the owner liable only for the amount that he or she contributed to the start-up of the company. With an LLC, the business structure allows for multiple members, so if the franchise owner wants to take on partners, she can do so under this type of organization. Each member is then financially responsible only for the initial amount that was contributed to the business. Furthermore, the LLC provides a fairly simple system of taxation. Instead of designating the business as a separate entity (as in a corporation), the LLC allows for "pass-through" taxation. In other words, the members can register profits and losses on their personal statements, instead of having to complete a separate tax statement for the business.

3. Corporation

A corporation functions as a unique legal entity, meaning that the business is separate from its owners. The separation removes the owners from any personal responsibility for debts that the business accrues, but it also removes them from the privilege of basic ownership. Within a corporation, the owners elect to become shareholders, and the corporation must then function under a separate board of directors. For small businesses like franchises, the S corporation; a variation of the standard corporation provides some flexibility for the owners. The S corporation is established similar to an LLC because the taxes pass through the corporation and can be filed on personal tax statements. In the S corporation, the owners are also allowed to designate a stated amount as income from the business, with any extra income that they received showing up as dividend from the company. In other words, an S corporation owner might make $100,000 in one year from the company, but he reports only $70,000 as income. The other $30,000 can be listed on the tax statement as dividend, which is not subject to employment taxes.

Chapter 4: Types of Franchise Methods

Franchising is a very complex area, but if you do your research properly and as a consequence manage to find the right franchise for you, it can be very rewarding. Before however you start to look at franchise opportunities of interest, you need to initially understand what franchising is and if it is the right route into business for you.

In simple terms, a "franchise" is an agreement between two parties which allows one party i.e. the franchisee, to market product or services using the trademark and operating methods of the other party i.e. the franchisor.

There are two types of franchise methods; business format franchising and product and trade name franchising.

Business Format Franchising

The most common method in the United Kingdom (UK) is Business Format Franchising. Using this method, when you buy a franchise, the franchisor grants you, the franchisee, the use of their logos and trademarks, as well as a turnkey system for doing business. This includes helping the franchisee with site selection, store layout and design, recruiting and training staff, marketing the business, preferred supplies contacts and more.

The franchisee in return has to pay an upfront franchise fee as well as ongoing royalties to the franchisor. The franchisor uses this money to help further develop the system through marketing, product and market research, and ongoing support.

There are many examples of business format franchising opportunities, including; food franchises, automotive franchises, estate agency franchises, retail franchises, recruitment franchises, children's franchises, coffee franchises, pet franchises, fitness franchises to name a few.

Many of these are ideal franchises for women, many are home-based franchises, part-time franchises and mobile franchises, and not all required a high level of investment, some are considered low-cost franchises.

Product and Trade Name Franchising

The other franchise method is Product and Trade Name Franchising. This type of franchising does not involve royalty fees. The most important thing that the franchisor provides to someone buying a franchise in Product and Trade Name Franchising is the product. The franchisee is required to purchase the product or range of products exclusively from the franchisor. The franchisor also provides national marketing and advertising campaigns, logos and trademarks.

This type of franchising is mainly associated with industries such as petroleum, soft drink distribution and automotive.

Product and Trade Name Franchising has three distinctive characteristics.

1. The franchisee sells goods which are supplied by the franchisor or a person affiliated with the franchisor.

2. The franchisor helps the franchisee to secure accounts or, depending on the type of business, locations or sites for rack displays or vending machines.

3. Within 6 months of opening the business, the franchisee must pay the franchisor or a person affiliated with the franchisor.

Chapter 5: Starting a Franchise Questions and Answers.

Keep in mind these requirements when you consider making the move from business owner to franchisor.

Question: I have got a great business that I think would be perfect for franchising. How do I get started as a franchise company? What kinds of advisors will I need and where do I find them? Is there a good source of information for me to start with?

Answer: Congratulations on building a successful business. It is exciting that you are considering using franchising as a method of expanding your brand and operations. You have some great questions so let's discuss each in turn.

First of all, one of the best starting points for researching this idea is the International Franchise Association (the IFA). The IFA is the industry trade association for franchising and has a host of resources that you can access to get started in this process. You can find the IFA and start your search by going to their website.

Starting a franchise company is not an easy or inexpensive process. There are a number of requirements you will have to meet and a few other things that, though not legally required, are also essential. These requirements includes.

1. Legal. You will be required to prepare a standard disclosure document for your franchise operation. This document, called the Uniform Franchise Offering Circular (UFOC) is required of all companies, by the Federal Trade Commission, if they want to offer franchises for sale anywhere in the United States. In addition, there are a number of individual states that have registration requirements you must meet if you are going to offer franchises in those states. You will need an effective and experienced franchise lawyer to help you meet these legal requirements correctly. As with any advisor, make sure to check the experience and references of lawyers when making this selection.

2. Accounting. You are going to need to prepare audited financial statements for the franchise company. This is actually one of the disclosure requirements under the legal section above so you won't be able to complete legal until you have your statements audited. You will have to decide if you want to set up another company to franchise your concept or if you want to use the existing business entity you are operating as your franchise company. You will need an experienced accountant to produce these audited statements and to advise you on the structure of your business enterprise. Again, make sure you are getting someone experienced in operating in the franchise arena and check references prior to deciding on this person.

3. Systems. The heart and soul of any successful franchise company is systems. You will need to develop and completely document the systems that a franchisee will use to run their business successfully. You will need to develop a training program that will teach a new franchisee whatever they need to know to become a successful operator. You will need to formalize the marketing plans that a new franchisee will use to drive customers into their new unit. You will also need to design a sales system that you can use to recruit new franchisees into your franchise company. There is a mountain of work getting all your systems set up and ready to go. You can hire outside consultants to assist with all this work but if you do, make sure you check references very carefully since there is a wide variance in terms of what these folks do and what they charge for it.

4. Mindset. One of the most important things you need to do in order to be a successful franchisor is to have the right focus and attitude. In your existing business, you are the boss, you have employees and they probably do what you tell them to do without much resistance. Franchisees are quite different from employees and you need to make sure you don't treat them as if they were employees. Successful franchisors use a lot of persuasion to get the franchisees to do what they want rather than issuing orders. It's not as fast or efficient but you will find that you meet a lot of resistance from franchisees if you don't do it this way. I don't know about specific advisors related to this topic but there are numerous industry meetings and opportunities for you to interact with other franchisors and you should take advantage of all these as a learning experience.

27

I will leave you with is a word of caution. Most honest advisors in the franchise business will tell you that you will need at least $100,000 to $500,000 in initial capital to even think about starting a franchise company. You will probably work harder than you ever have for at least 2-3 years before you even start to make any money on your franchise operations, and it could easily be 3-5 years.

The rewards and satisfaction of building a successful franchise company are incredible but so is the price that you will pay to reach this goal. Make sure that you want to pay the price before you start this process and then go forward with realistic expectations and you should do fine.

Question: How similar is starting a franchise to starting a conventional business.

Answer: You may well wonder whether the benefits of a standard start-up transfer to the world of franchising. It's worth remembering that a franchise is a hybrid between entrepreneurship and working for an established corporation. Therefore, aspects of both will be evident in the running of your franchise company.

We will compare each aspect of running a franchise and a company blow.

1. Raising finance: Although a franchisor will take much of the financial burden away from you compared with a conventional start-up, there are still significant initial costs to running a franchise. Of course, compared to starting up your own business, this kind of burden is relatively light. You are paying for a part of an established company's brand effectively ensuring a head start on someone starting from scratch. Depending on the franchise, all stock and equipment is likely to be supplied to you, along with premises and help with accounting and insurance.

There will be fewer commitments to soak up your money, allowing you to concentrate on improving the business. As for investment sources, you will rarely need to look further than your bank. With franchising being such a low-risk option, banks are generally very happy to lend money to franchisees, safe in the knowledge they will, at the very worst, have a parent company to chase if things go awry. Therefore, finding finance should be easier for a franchisee than a standard entrepreneur.

2. Support: Being a conventional entrepreneur means you have to live very much on your wits. There are arguably very few degrees that will teach you what the reality of running a business is like; if you haven't done it before, you will be taking a trip into the unknown. Also, the 'safety net' beneath entrepreneurs can vary greatly or not exist at all. Many people plough their entire savings behind a business that subsequently fails, leaving them with nothing when the debts mount up.

While friends and family can provide assistance with funding and advice, invariably your most important relationship will be with your bank manager.

Compared to a standard company, a franchise is a different story altogether. Almost all franchisors provide comprehensive training for their franchisees. Before taking on a territory, you should be given a full run-down of the market you will be working in, advice on any equipment you will be using and some help on business basics such as accounting, stocktaking and turnover projections.

Having been trained to run a fully-equipped business, the support doesn't end there. Most franchise companies offer their franchisees on-going help in the early days of the business and often put newcomers in touch with more experienced franchise owners for advice. When you consider the support franchisees enjoy compared with their start-up counterparts, it's easy to see why the sector has such a low failure rate.

3. Marketing and PR: As a start-up company, it's imperative that you get your message out there to the right audience. Through carefully targeted newspaper, online or radio advertising, you should be able to reach enough people to get some customers through your door. Next comes the ongoing process of building and maintaining a reputation. Get this right and you will begin to thrive from positive recommendations from satisfied punters.

It can be a long, time-consuming process and a costly one too; advertising isn't cheap and entrepreneurs often have to think up innovative, quirky ways in which to publicise themselves. As a franchisee, you will have the clout of a large, often well-known, brand behind you. You will be given all the marketing tools you need to spread the word about your business and will benefit from advertising, sometimes on a national level.

A large franchise company will have dedicated marketing departments that will be able to provide you with all the advice and materials required. Franchising provides you with plenty of support, but it isn't exactly the business equivalent of a blank canvas, unlike the experience of normal entrepreneurs. Franchisors have their own criteria on how each of their outlets should look and operate; however much; it feels like you are the ultimate boss on a day-to-day basis, you will always be working to someone else's vision, not your own.

The amount of freedom afforded to franchisees varies, but you will almost certainly be briefed on how the company wants to be represented, from the uniforms of staff to what suppliers to use. Also, should a franchisor change ownership or fail, the future of your franchise will be thrown into doubt. Likewise, the actions of your fellow franchisees will have an impact upon your image and, therefore, sales. It's important that you are comfortable with these circumstances before you purchase the franchise, or you could become extremely frustrated.

4. Making a profit: Franchising holds the upper hand here with one significant drawback. A franchise company will demand a percentage of the profits you achieve. They will also ask you to pay periodical fees to retain the franchise license, allowing you to continue trading. That said, your franchise will provide you with an ideal platform to make profits in the first place. You will be operating a proven business concept that has a solid reputation and a history of making money. You will be trained to run a business that is fully equipped, with most of the work done for you in terms of marketing and PR, meaning that many of the time and money consuming aspects of starting up a business will not be a factor when running a franchise. Moreover, it's likely the franchisor will have projections of how your business should grow, with practical advice on how to achieve profitability.

Chapter 6: Is Your Business Franchisable?

Franchising is a relatively flexible format, and just about any type of business can be franchised, provided it meets some basic characteristics.

1. It needs to be credible. Does your company have experienced management? A track-record over time?

2. Is the concept proven? Have you achieved good local press or public acclaim?

3. It needs to be unique. Is your business adequately differentiated from its competitors? Is it marketable as a business opportunity? Does it have a sustainable competitive advantage?

4. It needs to be teachable. Are the systems in place? Are operating procedures documented? Could someone learn to operate your business in three months or less?

5. It needs to provide an adequate return. I don't mean just profitability. If a business can't generate a 15 to 20 percent return on investment after deducting a royalty (typically between 4 and 8 percent), it's going to have difficulty keeping franchisees happy.

If your business meets these criteria, then it may be a good candidate for franchising.

When a company makes a decision to franchise, it must first develop a sound plan for expansion. This plan must take into consideration the numerous issues confronting a new franchisor; speed of growth, territorial development, support services, staffing and fee structure, to name just a few of the most important issues. Larger companies need to address more complex issues such as channel conflict, anti-trust issues, and resource allocation and obviously, your entire plan needs to be subjected to rigorous financial analysis and scrutiny to fine-tune your strategy for growth.

Once your plan is in place, you will need the proper legal documentation. At a minimum, you will need a franchise contract, an offering circular (as required under FTC Rule 436), and, depending on where franchises are being sold, state registrations. There are literally hundreds of different business issues that must be addressed in a good franchise agreement, and the decisions made regarding these issues will ultimately dictate your success as a franchisee.

Quality control for a new franchisor involves the development of highly developed systems. Generally, this translates into the development of an operations manual that must contain not only the systems used by the business, but also the checklists, policies, procedures and tactics that will allow these systems to be uniformly enforced. Moreover, operations manuals must be careful to avoid the creation of an agency and must also address issues that could create claims of negligence if you are to maintain an effective shield against consumer liability.

As a new franchisor, you must develop the ability to market and sell franchises. That requires knowledge of how to attract prospective buyers and the necessary materials (brochures, mini-brochures, videotapes, DVDs, and so on) that will help make the sale. Moreover, since the franchise sales process is highly regulated, you will need to be educated in proper sales, disclosure and compliance techniques.

Every new franchisor quickly learns that when they turn to franchising, they have entered a completely different business. Regardless of how you make money as a franchisor, you will have two roles; selling franchises and servicing franchisees and of the two, ensuring the success of your franchisees is the most important.

Properly structured, franchising can allow small companies to more effectively compete with much larger competitors. It can also allow larger companies to gain the advantages of highly motivated unit management while reducing overhead. As such, franchising is an option that more and more companies should explore.

The key to success in franchising is successful franchisees. Without successful franchisees, no franchise system will last. But if you can put the interests of your franchisee first, those same franchisees might help you become the next McDonald's.

Chapter 7: Should You Franchise Your business?

Though we believe that franchising is an excellent way of expanding an already successful business, we should point out that franchising is not right for every business.

So why franchise? Companies usually chose to franchise so that they can expand quickly, without huge outlay costs, to take advantage of opportunities that arise in the market.

The alternative to franchising is to do it yourself and open up shops/offices in certain geographical areas. You would then need to get managers in to run each shop/office whilst you oversee it. This could be hard to manage if you were not able to keep a tight control over them.

If you choose to franchise you would have independent people running their own business. They would be motivated to do well as they have a direct stake in the business.

How quickly do you want to expand and by how much? Franchising allows you to expand across cities, countries and continents. Do you want this level of awareness or are you happy just opening a few more units in your local area? You need to decide on what you want from the business and what level of expansion is needed.

Is your business right for franchising?

A business needs to be credible, it needs to have systems and procedures that can be replicated, as well as a concept that has sustainable unique selling points and is attractive to prospective franchisees and it must also be able to make both the franchisees and the franchisor money.

Only a successful business should franchise. Franchising is not the right way for a failing business to make money. You should only go down the franchise route if you already have a successful business up and running. If your business is new then you need to postpone franchising until you have an established track record.

Businesses need to have systems and procedures that can be copied by most people to run a successful business and it should also be replicated in various locations and not just suited to one particular region e.g. some foods can be specific to a particular region and not popular out of that region; what is popular in Florida may not be popular in Washington. When a business relies on the skills of individuals, then it is harder to franchise but not impossible e.g. optician franchisees. It is harder to franchise a skill-based business as you cannot teach people to quickly gain a highly qualified skill that someone has taken years of studying and learning to achieve.

Your business needs to have competitive advantages, i.e. Unique Selling Points (USP's) that makes it an attractive offer to both franchisors and to the marketplace. Some of the most popular and successful franchises are not necessarily the most exciting or attractive concepts, e.g. pest solution franchises, cleaning franchises, drainage franchises, but they have something that makes it an attractive option .e.g. unfortunately we are always going to have problems with pests so a pest solution franchise will always be in demand, as will cleaning and drainage. Does your franchise offer a service that is required and is resilient to changes in the market? Do you offer better support, marketing, pricing than your competitors?

You need to also have a business that when franchised will make money for you and your franchisees. The franchisee must be able to make enough money after they have paid their royalties to make a sufficient return on their investment.

You need to therefore firstly make sure that your business is right for franchising. If you do not have the right concept and attempt to franchise your business then it could fail, costing you a lot of money.

Chapter 8: Your Business May Be Right for Franchising But Are You?

You have identified that your business is franchiseable, but are you ready to take the step from manager to franchisor? How different can it be?!

Is becoming a franchise something you want to do or something you feel you should be doing? You need to want it and be passionate about growing the business via franchising.

As your business depends on the success of your franchisees and as franchisees are not employees of yours, you will need to treat them differently. This could mean changing how you build relationships and also how you manage people. You will be responsible for recruiting, managing and supporting people who have a vested interest in the business, and so you need to identify if you need to change how you manage and communicate.

You also need to be able to see what is right for your business in the long term and not be enticed to develop the business quickly when you start seeing the benefits of recruiting franchisees. If you develop too quickly you may not be able to support the franchisees sufficiently which can lead to conflict and negativity within the network. This can ultimately lead to failure.

The risks

You have now decided that the business and you are right for franchising, but what are the risks involved.

The biggest risk to any company looking to franchise their business is the cost. It is very expensive to franchise a business. Businesses can easily spend over $200,000 on areas such as preparing the legal documents, the operations manual, marketing materials, recruitment etc. This huge cost means that it can be extremely risky for businesses. You need to make sure that you are right for franchising before spending this amount of money.

Franchisors should however make this money back over time as they sign up franchises, in fact it could be as little as one franchisee needed for them to do this.

You should never be tempted to aim to sell as many franchisees as possible and as quick as possible to make your money back and more. This is a strategy used by unethical franchisors who are interested in using franchising as a "get rich quick" scheme. A good franchisor will be able to see the long term picture and know that they could actually make more money if they spent time developing the franchise properly.

Trying to sell franchises too quickly can also lead to greater costs being incurred e.g. you will need to market the opportunity which will cost money and you may need to hire additional staff to keep up with the demand created from your marketing activities.

Another risk of franchising your business is not recruiting the right franchisees. If you are not careful with the people you choose then it could lead to the downfall of your business. You need to make sure that you know exactly what you are looking for in a franchisee and take time to find franchisees who meet these requirements. It only needs to take one bad franchisee to cause a major negative impact on the franchise and your core business.

Chapter 9: Costs Involved in Opening a Franchise

You have to spend money to make money. So the old saying goes.

In franchising you can spend a lot or a little, and still make money. Once you have decided 1) that you want a franchised business, and 2) what industry segment you did like to work in (fast food, home repair, pet care, etc.), it's time to determine what you can afford. Your "budget" will limit your choices.

The cost of entry varies greatly, by both the segment you choose and the franchise brand you select within that segment. While costs range from less than $10,000 to upwards of $5 million, the majority of franchises run from about $50,000 or $75,000 to about $200,000 to get started.

Knowing how much you have to invest at the front end for the franchise fee and to set up your operation; whether a retail store with inventory and staff, or a home-based or mobile business with just one employee (you) allows you to focus realistically on which industries and which brands to consider.

At the low end, you can get into a home-based or mobile concept for $10,000 or less. At the high end are hotels, which can cost more than $5 million, including the land. Full-service restaurants run from about $750,000 to $3 million or more. Fast food restaurants cost from about $250,000 to $1 million and up. Auto repair and maintenance facilities run between $200,000 and $300,000. Note these are average ranges, and the cost of entry will vary from brand to brand.

Even before you sign a franchise agreement, you will incur costs such as professional fees (an attorney to review the contract and an accountant to work the numbers) and before you open, depending on the type of business you choose there will be costs for building out your store or office, inventory, equipment, insurance, employee training, business licenses, rent, landscaping, signage, etc. Buying your own real estate can be a significant, separate expense. Also be prepared for grand opening and initial advertising and promotional expenses. After you open there are ongoing expenses such as interest (if you have a loan), supplies, salaries, professional fees, rent, utilities, maintenance, uniforms, and more.

Then, of course, there is the franchise fee; the onetime entry price to use the franchisor's brand, operating system, and to receive ongoing support in management, training, marketing, and more. Franchise fees generally run in the $20,000 to $30,000 range, though they can top $100,000 for higher-end, more established brands. Once open, there are ongoing royalties to pay, which typically range from 4 percent to 8 percent of gross revenues and include an ongoing assessment for a joint marketing and advertising fund.

Franchisors usually have minimum financial requirements before seriously considering a candidate.

1. Liquidity: Unless you are printing money, your franchise business will take time to turn a profit (your franchisor should be able to tell you how long). Franchisors know this and usually require new franchisees to have a minimum amount of liquidity in order to keep the business afloat during its first year or more, until your bottom line turns from red to black.

2. Net worth: Franchisors also usually set a minimum level of net worth before they consider someone a true candidate for their brand.

For example, a Burger King will cost about $2.2 million for a typical restaurant; if you meet the minimum financial requirements of $1.5 million in net worth and $500,000 in liquid assets.

Entry cost also will vary based on the size (population) of the territory awarded and the level of services and support. For example, TSS Photography offers four different plans to potential franchisees, based on population and on the services, equipment, and training provided (territory cost ranges from $35,000 to $56,500). Another photography franchise, Clix!, offers two options. 1) a full studio version, from $218,725 to $381,040 (est.); and 2) an on-location (no studio) version from $36,235 to $77,510 (est.).

The franchise fee at Computer Medics of America is $5,000 for a population up to 150,000, and $20,000 for population of 850,000 to 1 million; after 5 years, a franchise fee of 25 percent of the initial fee is required to renew for 10 more years. At Nerd Force, which has a franchise fee of $12,000 for the first territory and $8,000 for each additional territory, total start-up costs range from $25,100 to $54,000 for a territory with an approximate population of 120,000.

An increasing number of franchisors offer discounts to veterans, minorities, and women. Incentives for vets, minorities, and women can include lower initial franchise fees and/or reduced royalty payments. At Nerd Force, for example, veterans receive a $4,000 discount off the initial $12,000 franchise fee; other franchisors offer discounts of 50 percent or more. Franchisors usually promote these incentives on their website. The IFA (International Franchise Association) website is a good place to learn more about these discounts and programs.

As the economy tightened in late 2008 and 2009, many franchisors began offering limited-time deals on franchise fees and royalties, deferred payments, money-back guarantees, and other promotional incentives. Some examples:

In March 2009, Port City Java announced a "No Royalty" promotion for the Carolinas under which any new franchisee will pay no royalties until 2011.

HomeVestors ("We Buy Ugly Houses") offered an "associate franchise" license for a $12,000, part-time, home-based program instead of $49,500 for its full-time, office-based format.

SKYshades offered a full refund of its $75,000 initial investment if new franchisees do not generate $1.5 million in revenue in their first three years. They are not alone in offering special incentives to attract new franchisees.

Although the entry costs and ongoing expenses of getting into franchising may seem steep, it also costs money to start your own business. One of the advantages of choosing a franchised business is that you enter with your eyes wide open regarding start-up and future costs. Based on the experience of existing franchisees, franchisors can provide you with a very accurate picture of what it will cost to start the business, your ongoing expenses, and a good approximation of when your revenue stream will turn positive; valuable information you won't have if you start your own business.

Chapter 10: Steps to Franchising Your Business

Franchising your business is a proven route to rapid growth. But becoming a franchisor is not an automatic ticket to success, especially in this challenging economy. For instance, three established franchisors filed for bankruptcy protection in the US; Taco Del Mar Franchising Corp., Uno Restaurant Holdings Corp., and Daphne's Greek Café.

Still, many business owners dream of seeing their brand become a household name, with a network of franchisees from coast to coast or around the globe. When the right concept is franchised effectively, it can be a great expansion strategy that doesn't require as much up-front capital as growing through company-owned units.

If you are considering franchising your business, know that the process of becoming a franchisor is usually long and involves considerable cost. Just because you qualify to sell franchises doesn't mean you will find buyers. Data from the International Franchise Association shows that of the 105 companies that started selling franchises in 2008, more than 40 had not reported the sale of their first unit by the end of 2009.

Becoming a successful new franchisor entails making many thoughtful decisions early on that will affect your business for years to come. There are also a lot of legal paperwork to wade through to make sure your business complies with federal and state laws that regulate the franchise industry.

Below are our thoughts on the important steps you will need to take along the road to becoming a new franchisor.

Step One: Evaluate if Your Business is Ready

The first question to ask is whether your business is suited to being franchised. Beyond having a track record of sales and profitability at the existing business, there are several factors to weigh here.
.

a. Consider your concept.

Most good franchise concepts, offer something familiar, but with some unique twist to it. A good example is Florida-based Pizza Fusion which offers a familiar product; pizza but with all organic ingredients, delivered in hybrid-electric cars.

The concept has to appeal both to end consumers and to prospective franchisees. There should be an expectation that more units will create economies of scale and increase profits. Additionally, the business needs to be something you can systematize and replicate, not something that needs your personal touch to be successful.

"Ask yourself, is the concept sellable?" "Can you clone it? Does it provide good returns?

b. Check your financials.

Most successful franchises take a business that is already profitable and try to replicate that success in other locales. A franchise consultant once says she likes to see companies with at least a couple of profitable units beyond the first one already in operation before a company tries franchising.

c. Gather market research.

Don't rely on your gut feeling that your business would be a smash hit across the country. Gather market research to confirm there is widespread consumer demand beyond your home city for what your franchise business would offer, and room in the marketplace for a new competitor.

d. Prepare for change.

Becoming a franchisor means you will be engaged in entirely different activities than you were as a business owner. You will primarily be selling franchises and supporting franchisees now, instead of selling pizza or fixing toilets.

Ask yourself if you are comfortable having a role as a teacher and salesperson, selling and supporting franchisees, as opposed to going out there and doing it yourself.

In addition, franchising your business will require that you relinquish some of the control you have had over how your concept is executed.

Franchisees won't do it exactly the way you would, even if they do it well. If you are so married to your concept that you won't let anyone else touch it, then franchising may not be right for you.

e. Evaluate other alternatives.

Before you plunge into franchising, you may want to consider other options. Depending on your situation slower growth, finding debt financing or taking on partners are all alternatives that may prove better ways to move forward.

It also can cost $100,000 or more, so ask yourself if your company has the financial resources. Remember that while franchising allows you to grow fast, it also means giving up most of the franchise units' future profits.

Step Two: Learn the Legal Requirements

In order to legally sell franchises anywhere in the United States, your business must complete and successfully register a Franchise Disclosure Document with the Federal Trade Commission . In the FDD, you will be asked to provide a wide range of information about your business, including audited financial statements, an operating manual for franchisees, and descriptions of the management team's business experience.

Beyond the federal FDD requirements, some states have their own rules for selling franchises within their borders. California and Illinois are generally regarded as having the most daunting registration process. If you want to sell in one of these states, you will need to meet their requirements as well, at additional cost.

Franchisor Cindy Deuser, Co-founder of franchisor Lillians Shoppes, says the rule binder her home state of Minnesota provided was two inches thick. It took the bargain-fashion-accessory company a full year and cost more than $100,000 to qualify in 45 of the 50 states, she reports.

"It took longer than we thought, and was very intense in terms of all the things you have to cover," she says.

To advise and assist in this process we recommend that you hire an experienced franchise consultant or franchise lawyer. Often, a new company will be set up to act as the franchisor. Find an expert who can make sure you are doing every required step correctly.

Step Three: Make Important Decisions About Your Model

As you prepare your legal paperwork, you will need to make many decisions about how you will operate as a franchisor. Key points include.
    a. The franchise fee and royalty percentage.
    b. The term of your franchise agreement.
    c. The size territory you will award each franchisee.
    d. What geographic area you are willing to offer franchises within.
    e. The type and length of training program you will offer.

f. Whether franchisees must buy products or equipment from your company.
g. The business experience and net worth franchisees need.
h. How you will market the franchises.
i. Whether you want an owner-operator for each unit or area/master franchisees who will develop multiple units

New franchisors don't realize how much each of these decisions can affect their future profitability.

If you are thinking either 5 percent or 6 percent royalty, for instance, the difference doesn't sound big but five years later, when you have 100 franchises sold, and they each make $700,000 a year, that's a $7 million annual mistake and you have signed a 10-year contract.

Lillians' Deuser says she and her sister/partner Sue Olmscheid, ran many business-model scenarios with their franchise attorney before settling on their $25,000 franchise fee, 7-1/2 percent royalty and 10 year contract term. They seem to have hit a winning formula. Lillians grown to over 33 shops in its first two years as a franchisor with its unique concept, in which stores are only open a few days a month.

Be careful to note whether geographic variables such as weather or local laws may affect franchisees' success. Territory size is important too, as too-large territories may have to be bought back later at a premium so they can be split up.

In the case of San Francisco Bay-area solar-panel installation franchisor Solar Universe, the company is selling franchises in concentric circles moving outward from its headquarters, mostly in warm-weather states with high electricity costs and generous state green-energy rebates.

Inadequate training can leave your franchisees ill-equipped to implement your system successfully. Solar Universe spent nearly $1 million preparing to franchise, including $150,000 to create a state-of-the-art training centre for franchisees complete with indoor roofs where they can practice installations.

Step Four: Create Needed Paperwork and Register as a Franchisor

Once you have made the important decisions that shape how your franchise will operate, you are ready to complete your legal paperwork. When you submit it, be prepared for authorities to critique the document and possibly demand additional disclosures before they approve your application.

While the FTC essentially just files your FDD away, you will need to wait for state approval. Solar Universe waited several months to receive comments back from the state of California on its filing, and it took four months in all to get approved there.

Step Five: Make Key Hires

As you prepare to become a franchisor, you will usually need to add several staff members who will focus solely on helping franchisees. In the case of Solar Universe, the company sells its franchisees the solar panels they use, so founder Bono says he needed a full-time hire to staff the order desk. The company also hired a trainer and a full-time "franchise advocate" to answer franchisee questions and resolve any problems.

For its part, Lillians Shoppes hired a trainer, a creative director, a marketing assistant and a franchise-process manager who helped get franchisees using company software and systems, says CEO Deuser. Lillians. The founding sisters still do all the buying for the growing chain, but Deuser says growth means they are already looking into hiring a second trainer.

Step Six: Sell Franchises

Now that you are in business as a franchisor, one of your most pressing activities will be to find franchisees and convince them to buy your concept. Lillians is unusual in that the company has sold all its franchises by word of mouth and doesn't have a sales representative. To help stimulate interest, the company offers a $1,000 referral fee to anyone who sends the company a new franchisee. At Solar Universe, they hired two in-house salespeople to handle franchise marketing.

Selling franchises is difficult because of the high risk involved for franchisees. Your salespeople should know your business well and be able to tell a compelling story about why you worth the investment of their time and money.

You are saying, I want you to give me all your money; then, quit your job, give up your security and benefits, and go into a business you have never been in before and follow my rules. You will need to establish a pretty high level of trust.

Step Seven: Support Franchisees

As a franchisor, you will have gone through a lot to reach this point. But here is the point where you begin to support your franchisee network; is where a chain ultimately succeeds or fails. Your training programs and other support efforts will create quality control and making sure the brand provides a uniform experience no matter which unit customers visit. With the Internet, this has increasingly come to mean providing ongoing online learning modules for franchisees to use.

If you are a restaurant operator and employ 20 people in a unit, you have thousands of new employees going through the system every year. Without ongoing training, it's pretty easy to institutionalize wrong behaviours.

At the same time, you will need to start marketing the growing chain to drive sales to franchisees. Many new franchisors underestimate how much this marketing and support effort will cost. Marketing encompasses everything from radio or print ads to uniforms, logos, fliers, and logo art on company vans. You are going to need a lot of money for marketing.

Chapter 11: Questions for the Franchisor

When looking to buy the right franchise, you must have confidence in the franchisor you choose and ask them questions about their business and the structure of their organisation at the early stages.

Below are some questions to ask before buying a franchise to help you assess the franchise opportunity. Please bear in mind that there are many types of franchises and you may have to tailor these questions to suit the specific franchise you are enquiring about, e.g. if you are looking to buy a food franchise, your questions will be different from those you would ask if buying a home-based franchise.

1. What is the background of all the directors? Have they got franchising experience? Why did they decide to go down the franchise route?

2. Are they financially sound? Have they ever been bankrupt?

3. What is the total cost to buy a franchise? Will you supply me with a breakdown of all costs necessary to open the business? What are these costs?

4. Are there any other costs I can expect to be asked for after I open the franchise? Do I have to contribute to any other costs such as advertising and

promotional expenditure that you incur, if so how much?

5. Do you charge ongoing franchise fees and if so what are they and how are they calculated?

6. Do I have to pay a deposit or upfront payment, and if I do not proceed will I lose my deposit or any part of it?

7. How much working capital would I need, and what help can you give me in estimating my projections?

8. What is my expected break even and how long should it take me to reach this figure?

9. How long will it take to start trading from the time I sign the contract?

10. How thorough is the training at the start-up stage and thereafter? What will the training consist of and how long will it last? Are all training costs included in my franchise fee?

11. What help, if any, will I receive if I want to do some advertising and promotion on my own?

12. After I have opened my franchise what ongoing support am I provided with?

13. What help and guidance do you offer in site selection?

14. Do you provide instructional and operational manuals and can I see them prior to signing?

15. Can I be provided with a full list of all franchisees in the network and can I contact them?

16. How many franchisees have you opened in the past 12 months? How many do you plan to open in the next 12 months?

17. How successful is the franchise and the existing franchisees? Can you tell me about the best and worst performing franchisee?

18. How thoroughly do you vet prospective franchisees to maintain a high standard in the network? How many do you reject?

19. Have any franchisees failed, and if so why?

20. How do you handle grievances with existing franchisees?

21. Will the territory offered be for my sole and exclusive use?

22. Are you currently operating in areas with similar demographics as my proposed territory?

23. Does your company see any threats in the current marketplace?

Though this is a good array of questions to ask when buying a franchise business, it is not an exhaustive list and so you should expand on any areas you wish more clarification on.

Chapter 12: Franchise Considerations

You have done your homework and researched franchising and now want to buy a franchise, but is it the right route into self-employment for you? Though franchising is a very appealing business start-up option; however, it is not for everyone. Before you decide to go down the franchise route and start to consider franchises to buy, you need to identify if franchising is right for you.

Below is a list of questions you can ask yourself. Asking these should give you a better understanding as to whether you could be a franchisee and will help you answer the question, "should I buy a franchise business?". You should also discuss them with your partner or family members as their input could be invaluable.

Question:
What physical condition are you in? Are you healthy? Do you suffer from any illnesses that could affect your ability to run your own business?

Suggestion:
Franchising is more than a 9-5 job. It is your business so you will need to put in long hours and work weekends if required. If you are not in good health or suffer from an illness that could affect how you perform as a business owner, then franchising may not be for you.

Question:
How much of your assets are you willing to risk in a franchise business?

Suggestion:
You need to calculate the value of your assets including savings, redundancy pay, car, house etc, and then work out how much you can risk losing. You will need to put a lot of your own capital into the business; can you afford to lose this? Can your family afford to lose it? What will happen if you do lose all your money? This is the worst case scenario but one you need to consider.

Question:
How much working capital can you afford to put into the business? What are your current financial commitments i.e. do you have a mortgage, loans, bills etc. If you had a drop in income, which can be common at the start of a business venture, could you afford this?

Suggestion:
During the early months of new business cash flow problems may result in income from the business being lower than expected. Are your financial commitments such that you could manage on less income than you have now?

Question:
Is your partner or family willing to give you full support? Are they happy to share the risks with you?

Suggestion:

There are always problems and difficult periods even in a successful franchise, and it is during these times that you may need a bit more family support than usual. It may be an idea to ask them to list their concerns so you can look at them in more detail.

Question:

Is your partner or family aware of the disruption to the family life that starting a new business can bring? This disruption could range from a few missed meals to the abandonment of an annual holiday and the working of long hours. Ask them for reactions to these possibilities.

Suggestion:

You should of course have discussed the franchise idea fully with your partner. Many franchisors positively encourage the involvement of spouses or partners in their discussions with franchisees; but you should also ask yourself whether your relationship would stand the strain of the sacrifices, which are inevitably involved in starting your own business. Be sure your partner is not going along with your ideas just to make you happy; make sure he or she is as committed as you are.

Question:

How many extra hours above a standard 40 hour week would you be prepared to work as a franchisee?

Suggestion:

As you will be aware, running a franchise could involve you in much more than a 9.00am to 5.00pm, weekday job. You may have said that you would be willing to work 20 or more hours extra. Is this realistic; what would you give up in a week to work those extra hours? If you said 2 or 3 hours or more, do you really have the commitment necessary to succeed in a new venture? It is your business and you will be responsible for all your decisions you have to spend all of the hours necessary to make the business work.

Question:
What reaction would you have to receiving strict guidelines by the franchisor on how to run your business?

Suggestion:
If you value a high degree of autonomy and want to make your own decisions on how to run and develop business, then franchising is possibly not for you. The franchisor is in ultimate control and resentment of this in your part will make the relationship very difficult.

Question:
What involvement would you expect from the franchisor in resolving problems encountered in running the franchise?

Suggestion:
Although the franchisor should help you with certain types of problems, do not expect assistance with all your minor difficulties. If you expect a large degree of assistance you should choose a franchise very

carefully, selecting one which is well established and with well-defined systems for operating the business.

Question:

If you see improvements could be made to the environment in which you work, how determined would you be to change them for the better?

Suggestion:

In running a franchise business, you will be expected to go by the rules, not change them. A franchisor will object vigorously if you try to 'personalise' the business. If you will be unable to resist making changes, then think again?

Question:

What would be your reaction to do tasks, such as serving food or cleaning tables?

Suggestion:

You may need to do a lot of the dirty work yourself, particularly in the early days. If you don't want to get involved, make sure that profit margins are sufficiently high to enable you to take on staff.

Question:

In your present employment are you used to taking financial decisions?

Suggestion:

The franchisor will be concerned if you have had little or no financial experience. Are you convinced that you have the necessary financial skills and knowledge?

Question:
Do you think you have the talent and skills that is required to market and sell your service or product?

Suggestion:
Similarly, are you capable of selling and marketing your business? Are you sufficiently creative? A franchisor will be reassured if you have had some experience.

Question:
How good do you think you are at motivating staff?

Suggestion:
If you have had problems with staff in the past and have blamed them, are you sure the problems were with the staff and not in the way that you dealt with them? Again, some franchisors may be concerned if you have had no experience of staff management.

Question:
Have you had frequent changes in jobs?

Suggestion:
If the answer to this question is yes, are you sure that franchising is something you really want to commit yourself to and that you aren't just looking for yet another change? On the other hand, if you haven't moved jobs a few times in your career, are you sure that you are suited to the different lifestyle, which you may face?

Question:

What are your feelings on job security? Some people like a lot of job security, whilst for others this is not important.

Suggestion:

Think carefully if you don't like insecurity, are you prepared to give up the comfort of receiving a regular wage.

So if you are considering buying a franchise, guidelines like these will help you answer the question "should I buy a franchise business?"

Chapter 13: Finding the Right Franchise Opportunity

When looking to buy a franchise, one of the most common questions we get asked is "what is the best franchise in the United Kingdom (UK)?". The problem is; there is no correct answer. It is probably the same as asking: 'what's the best car to buy?' There are so many points to consider, for instance; how much do you want to spend? What type of roads will you be driving on? How many passengers will you take? Do you want a new car or a used one? Does the insurance premium matter?

Like when buying a car, there are many questions to answer before you can reach a shortlist of franchises to buy. The best franchise for you may not be the best franchise business for someone else.

Just like the questions you need to address about your ideal car, there are similarly questions to ask yourself when buying a franchise.

1. What type of work do you like to do?
2. What type of work are you good at?
3. Are there any particular franchise industries that interest you?
4. Do you want to work in an office or do you prefer to work from home?
5. Would you prefer to be mobile and spend a lot of time travelling to meet clients?
6. How many hours and which hours do you want to work e.g. daytime, weekends, flexible?

7. Do you prefer to work by yourself or in a team?
8. Are you happy managing people?
9. Are you happy dealing with the public?
10. Would you be comfortable in a role that focuses on making sales?
11. How much money do you want to invest?
12. How far are you willing to travel to work each day?

And many, many more questions that you may or may not know the answer to should be considered when looking to buy a franchise, but answering these will help you get a better idea of what you want to do and will also assist you in narrowing down the options available to you.

When you have decided what you like doing and what you are best at doing, only then can you start exploring the many franchise opportunities that cover your personal preference. Remember it is so very important that you choose the type of franchise that allows you to do the type of work that you like and are good at for two important reasons. Firstly if you like what you do and are good at it, you will be more likely to succeed and secondly, buying a franchise is not something that you can step out of lightly. You need to consider working at the franchise at least for the next five years so it is important that you are happy doing the work involved.

Franchising is not easy, but it is a safer way to owning your own business. It is a tried and tested business format; someone else has made the mistakes for you so you don't have to and you are able to see the business in operation before investing any money.

You may want to buy a franchise, but is franchising right for you? To be a successful franchisee you would have to be the type of person who can accurately stick to someone else's system, without wanting to make changes. You will be starting your business using someone else's know-how and expertise gained over years of running a mirror image business and on top of it you don't have to worry about developing the system. The franchisor does that; you will however have to manage, promote, market and sell as well as millions of other tasks that have to be done in running small businesses.

Which type of franchise suits you best?

In order to find which franchise is best for you, you must assess your own skills and experiences. Once you have found the type of work that suits you best you can then select the franchise type that suits you. You should also consider what risks you are prepared to take, although the risks in franchising are different to those involved in setting up your own business.

What type of experience do you have?

Identify the skills you have developed over the years in order to ensure the franchise you chose fits your skills and experiences.

Have you managed staff? Many franchisees are geared to a franchise employing many staff with managed skills.

Have you been involved in administration? Many franchise systems involve extensive administration work therefore it would be beneficial to have some experience in this area.

Where do you want to work?

You need to ask yourself what type of environment you wish to work in:
a) Do you want to work in a shop?
b) Do you want to work in an office?
c) Do you want to work from home?
d) Do you want to be mobile and travel to customers?

What do you enjoy doing?
a) Talking on the phone?
b) Motivating people?
c) Working with your hands?
d) Driving?
e) Direct selling?
f) Talking face-to-face with customers?
g) Administration?
h) Managing people?
i) Working with children?
j) Working with animals?
k) Numbers, accountancy?
l) Multi-tasking?

When you are awarded a franchise, you are committing yourself to operating the business for at least five years. If you don't enjoy the work, you will be miserable.

Our advice is to find a franchise that you will enjoy working at and is comfortably within your skill set. For example, if you are an introvert and hate selling, don't consider a sales orientated franchise; however, always remember that business does not happen until a sale is made, so if you don't want to sell, maybe you are not cut out for business. The key thing is to be realistic and aim for something you will enjoy. The franchise you select should match your specific skills.

Chapter 14: Evaluating the Franchise

When buying a franchise it is imperative that you take as much franchise advice as possible. You need to look at a number of important areas in more detail.

Information

The first step is to assess the franchisor and its business. When you take up a franchise you are entering into a long term business relationship and it is very important that you spend some time looking into the background and performance of your prospective partner.

These enquiries should be backed up by financial information on the franchisor, including the audited accounts. Your accountant will comment on the accounts for you and a bank reference on the franchisor, obtained for you by your bank, might be helpful.

Information on the performance of the existing franchisees should be forthcoming and the franchisor should be willing to let you have a full list of franchisees to whom you can talk to or visit.

In the case of a new franchise you should look carefully at the performance of the pilot operation. Then there is the nature of the franchise business itself; you should ascertain whether or not there is a market for the products or services in your chosen area and what the future market is likely to be.

Support

So having established the soundness of the franchisor and the business you should then look at the strengths and weaknesses of the franchise operation. Critical to your likely success or failure is the level of support and training available from the franchisor, both at start up and subsequently.

There should be a comprehensive operations manual which gives you guidance on all aspects of running the franchise operation. An important aspect to consider is what help, if any, does the franchisor give in respect of any staff recruitment and training you may have to undertake.

Legal Contract

The next step is to consider the legal implications of the franchise contract.

As this document will be legally binding once you have signed it, you should receive a copy well in advance. We strongly recommend that you obtain independent legal advice on the contract from a solicitor well versed in franchise agreements, preferably a British Franchise Association affiliate.

Financing

Having got this far, and assuming you still wish to proceed, the next step is to examine the financial aspects of the franchise. Broadly speaking, these fall into two categories; the start up costs and the hoped for income/profits. Looking at the start up costs first, it is important that you identify the total amount of money required to get the business started, including any 'working capital' needed.

Against this sum will be set the amount of cash you can put into the venture, leaving the sum you will need to borrow. You will then have to consider what assets, if any, you or the business might have available as security for the required loan.

You must be prepared to take a realistic view of what might be a practical possibility in borrowing terms; whilst unsecured borrowing might be possible in some circumstances for a good franchise it is, for example, unlikely you can borrow say £90,000 towards a franchise costing £100,000, especially if you have no security. Having established the start up costs and borrowing requirements, you will then have to look at the potential earning power of the business on a realistic basis. Does it justify the level of investment and can you recover your investment?

Projections

Having satisfied yourself on these points you will have to get down to the detail, ensuring that any profit forecasts and cash flow forecasts prepared by the franchisor for your franchise are sensible.

This is also a good opportunity to look closely at matters, such as how the franchisor takes its income and what other fees may be payable. The last hurdle then remaining is to take the projections and your business plan to your bank and to convince them to lend you the money!

One final point. Whilst the steps outlined above might appear time consuming and tedious, you must remember that taking on a franchise is likely to be a very important and major step in your life. So it is worth taking the time to assess the franchise properly and get as much professional advice as possible on how to do so.

Chapter 15: Evaluate the Franchise Market

If you are buying a franchise opportunity, you are going to be working, selling and promoting the product or service for a long period of time. You can't change or develop the product or service, so make sure that the franchise has long term appeal and its market is not threatened in any way.

It is important that the franchisor can demonstrate a clear understanding of the future market for the product or service and that you both clearly understand the following.

Question:
Is the market for this product/service expanding rapidly, growing slowly, static or declining?

Suggestion:
The more advertisements you see for the product or service now than a couple of years ago can give you an indication of the state of the market

Question:
Does the product/service have special features which help it to sell? Does it warrant a premium price?

Suggestion:
In order to make money for the franchisee and franchisor, the product has to have real advantages over competitors. It may be difficult to maintain

premium prices if the product or service could be easily copied by others.

Question:
Who would your competitors be and how competitive would your product or service be in relation to them?

Suggestion:
Do competitors have any technical or price advantages? Could you improve on the service offered? What is their level of advertising? If there are no competitors ask yourself why there are none.

Question:
You have looked at the general market for your product, what do you know of the local market in which you will be operating?

Suggestion:
Does the local market have the same characteristics as the market in general? Is the product particularly suitable for your area? How dependent is success of the business on particular lifestyles or levels of income?

Chapter 16: Joining a Franchise

Understanding the Process of Joining a Franchise and why it's a two-way street.

Becoming a franchisee is not a case of 'sign here and cheque please' at least, if it is, then you should run away quickly!

Every good franchisor has in-depth, rigorous selection processes; equally, any decent franchisor will allow you to interview the company as much as the company interviews you. Joining a network is a two-way process; the franchisor is assessing your suitability at the same time as you are gauging the opportunity on offer.

Robust franchisee recruitment procedures ensure that both parties fully understand each other and that you are happy with the commitments, systems, support and operations that you are signing up to.

So what should you expect from a good franchisee recruitment process?

What to look for as a prospective franchisee.

1. Quality control

Franchisees share a brand with other business owners. You want to ensure that the others are just as conscientious about the standards and growth of the brand as you are; therefore be wary of any franchise that doesn't seem that worried about how suitable you are for the business.

2. Franchising background

A franchisor might be relatively new to the sector or might be a veteran of many years, but they should be honest about what their experience of franchising is. Ask about how long they have been running the business, how long they have been franchising, and any difficulties they have faced along the way.

3. The people

You will need to forge close relationships with the people behind the brand, especially in the early days of getting your franchise operational, when support is usually more intensive. You want to be sure that you trust them and can envision working with them; it will make life a lot easier for both of you in the longer-term.

4. Recruitment rates

Ask about how many franchisees have been recruited in the last 12 months and how many more they are looking to recruit in the next 12 months. What is important is the right level of support for the network, now and in the future. Good franchisors understand it's about sustainability, not just a race to the biggest number; many brands purposefully recruit very limited and carefully measured numbers of franchisees per year, to ensure support remains at optimum levels as the network expands.

5. Franchisee access

Networking with existing franchisees is one of the best resources for your research. Don't accept just one handed to you by the franchisor; what is to say that they are not the only successful franchisee? Ask for a full list and try to speak to as many as possible and get a realistic view of what life is like in the network.

6. Failure rates

Less than 5% of franchises close through commercial failure each year, so it's uncommon; but just about every network will experience a failure at some point; unfortunately franchising is not a guarantee. What is important is why franchisees fail; has the market changed; is there sufficient support; is it because the system doesn't work; or is it that the franchisee simply didn't put in the required level of work?

7. Visit their head office

Meet the franchisor at their office, which could be anything from a home-based centre of operations to a large corporate HQ. Either way it will help better inform you about the business and whether it matches with what they have told you to date.

8. Get legal documents checked

It is common practice to be asked to sign a non-disclosure document; however, don't sign it unless you have fully read and understood it. You will also get a franchise agreement, which is the legally-binding contract between franchisor and franchisee. Do not sign this until you have had it checked by a professional franchise lawyer.

In the United Kingdom; there is no franchise-specific legislation, making the sector a specialist and niche field of legal expertise in the context of general business law. Taking the wrong advice from an unsuitably experienced adviser can prove extremely expensive.

9. Deposits

You may be asked to pay a deposit during the recruitment process, which is standard practice for many franchisors. This is refundable if you decide not to progress things further, minus any reasonable costs incurred. Get a receipt and check the conditions carefully before paying any deposit.

What you should expect from a potential franchisor.

1. Timescales

The entire recruitment process in franchising is never just an hour-long meeting in a coffee shop or bar. Depending on the network and date of your enquiry, the whole process could range from a couple of weeks through to a year. If the process is lengthy and substantial, try not to get frustrated; instead, see it as a good quality check.

2. Getting personal

Don't be surprised if your spouse, partner or a family member are invited to attend meetings with you. Franchisors frequently want to really understand you as a person and part of that can be to see if the people around you are supportive of your decision, which can be a crucial factor in business success. They will want to know what you want from the business

Be sure about why you are going into franchising. Is there something you are looking to achieve? Having a clear mind about this during the interview process will help you in your conversations with the franchisor, who will expect you to know.

3. Exit strategy
Don't be surprised if as part of the interview process you are asked whether you have thought about a long-term plan to leave the franchise! Some franchisors like to see if you have a plan or goal that you are working to, such as 15 years to build the business then sell and retire. You may not have a clue at this stage, but it's worth thinking about it as it will help you plan what you are looking to achieve.

4. Testing times
Some franchisors conduct psychometric tests on their prospects to help them assess suitability; others might ask you to spend time shadowing a current franchisee. Almost all have their idea about what makes a suitable, successful franchisee, including their background and transferable skills, so these are not things to be feared but treated as a valuable part of the process.

5. Questions, questions, questions
Don't be afraid to ask difficult questions. Good franchisors will be encouraged if they see that you are taking this seriously and won't want you to go any

further if you are not clear about what you are committing to.

Perhaps the most valuable advice is to make sure that you take your time in the recruitment process. It's a serious commitment that requires serious consideration, and treating it as such will see you in a much better position to start building your own thriving business once you have found the right franchise for you.

Chapter 17: What a Franchisor Looks for in a Franchisee

When looking to recruit franchisees, franchisors consider the follow characteristics to be important in a franchisee.

1. They should be highly motivated and with a strong desire and passion to be successful.

2. They should display confidence and enthusiasm for what they are selling.

3. They should have the ability to motivate themselves and others.

4. They should be a quick learner and be able to pass their skills and knowledge on to their staff.

5. They should be able to express a good knowledge of the business and the industry in which they would be operating.

6. They should possess excellent management and sales skills, and demonstrate a high level of customer service.

The franchisor tends to prefer getting someone who doesn't necessary have experience in their industry. This is due to them wanting to train the franchisee in all aspects of their business and how they do things, instead of inheriting processes and methods picked up elsewhere. If the franchisee does run the business differently from how the franchisor wants it run, then this could lead to conflict and problems.

In the same note, franchisors tend to like to get franchisees who may not necessarily posses a high level of entrepreneurial skills and who are not competent in starting and building a business by themselves as they want to train and support them.

Chapter 18: Reasons for Getting into Franchising

Franchising can be a great way of starting a business and with hundreds of franchise opportunities on offer, we will discuss why it might be the right option for you...

Earlier this year, a Franchise Survey found that United Kingdom (UK) franchise businesses are performing at their best since the country entered recession in 2008.

Assessing the franchise sector from 2008 to 2014, the survey suggested that the industry had grown by 20% in comparison to a 2.5% increase in the economy overall, and found franchise employment to be at an all-time high with over 250,000 jobs created in the last 12 months.

But how much money can you make from franchising? Turnover for franchise brands across England and Wales was also reported to be at its highest since 2008 with Wales reporting a record 33% increase, the north west growing by 27%, the north east by 14%, and the south east by an impressive 42%.

Franchising continues to be a dependable business opportunity and UK franchisors and franchisees are confident about the future, with nine out of 10 franchisors reporting optimism for trading conditions over the coming year.

Given these findings, it's easy to see why franchising is an attractive option for those of you thinking 'I want to start my own business' but who would prefer the security of a well-known brand.

Here are 10 top reasons to choose franchising over starting a business from scratch

1. Franchising provides a variety of businesses you can buy into and has something for everyone.

2. Franchised businesses range from multi-million pound operations to part-time businesses run from a bedroom so there is something for every budget.

3. Franchising has been proven to be one of the safest ways of starting a new business compared to other business start-ups. But how profitable is franchising? In the a 2014 Franchise Survey; 92% of franchisees reported profitability and an impressive 80% of new franchisees who launched in the last two years were already turning a profit.

4. Franchising is a means of starting and running your own business with a very high success rate, provided you choose a good franchise in the first place.

5. A good franchise will offer you a proven business format with initial and continuing support. Franchisors often have field support staff to help franchisees.

6. Your business will operate under an already-established brand that has been developed and proven in the marketplace and the franchisor continues to research market demands so you don't have to.

7. Franchising gives you the opportunity to build a profitable business that can be resold, if you choose to.

8. You don't have to come up with the business idea; someone already has and tested it so you don't have to make any expensive mistakes. You should receive a comprehensive operations manual and training programme as part of the franchise agreement.

9. The franchisor has a marketing, sales and advertising strategy to promote the franchise network so you benefit from a holistic approach.

10. As part of a franchise; you benefit from network buying power so your costs are less, plus you have greater access to finance because banks look favourably on the franchise sector.

Chapter 19: Applying for a Franchise

You should determine which franchise opportunities might suit you and then you should contact the franchisors for further information. Narrow down your list of possibilities to two or three companies, using an initial evaluation of the franchisors, their products and services, and their franchise opportunities.

In order to conduct a meaningful investigation of your choices as a potential franchise owner, you should explore more than one franchise company in great detail. You may have sent an initial request for information to 10 or 15 companies, but you can't do an in-depth evaluation of all of them and you won't need to. In most cases, you can tell right away whether or not you are really interested in knowing more about a given franchise. By answering the following basic questions about each franchise that has immediate appeal for you, you will be able to pinpoint two or three real possibilities from among those that you initially thought might interest you.

1. Would you enjoy making a career out of running this franchise?
2. Do you have the skills or could you learn them to be able to operate this franchise business?
3. Do you have the resources to invest in and operate this franchise?

4. Does it seem as if the returns of your investment in this franchise might be in line with your financial needs and objectives?
5. Does the franchisor appear reputable, forthcoming, and the type of company with which you would enjoy a partnership?

Checking off the above points will help you decide which franchisors you would like to know more about. As you continue your franchise investigation, don't rely solely on the information companies send to you.

The franchise interview

As all franchise systems are different, franchisors will look for different required skills and characteristics depending on the nature of the business.

The franchise interview is where the franchisor decides if you are right for their business, and equally where you decide if the franchise is right for you. Remember it is a two-way interview and whilst you need to sell yourself to the franchisor, they should be selling themselves to you. Use the interview to find out everything you need to know about the franchise.

We have outlined below some common attributes that franchisors look for and how you should present yourself in the interview.

1. Wear business attire. We know it sounds obvious but people still query what to wear in an interview. You should always go formal unless asked not to by

the franchisor. The way you present yourself gives the franchisor an indication of how you would represent the company. No franchisor would hire someone who looked scruffy in the interview! It is not just about how you look but how you present yourself. Be professional at all times and come across in a positive light.

2. You need to be willing to follow the franchisor's system. The franchisor has spent years building their system so that is operating successfully as a franchise; they do not want someone to come in and start suggesting changes to it. You should demonstrate in the interview that you have a good grasp of how the system works and that you are keen to be part of it.

3. Be able to express why your skills meet those required by the business. What experience do you have? What are your skills? Why you would be an asset to the franchise. Show your business acumen.

4. Show the franchisor that you know about their industry. Research it before you go so that you can impress them with stats etc. Ask questions about the competition and any threats or weaknesses, strengths or opportunities you have identified, talk about any of the company's promotion you have seen and what you liked about it. It is ok to ask questions but do not interrogate them about negatives as it will only make the franchisor defensive.

5. Demonstrate your knowledge of the area you are interested in. Tell them why you think you can make

the franchise a success in this area. Reveal any community initiatives you are involved in.

6. Display to the franchisor where you are getting the money for the franchise.

Chapter 20: Key Steps in Opening a Franchise

Opening your own franchise business is a BIG step for those who choose the venture and it can be somewhat intimidating. The franchise marketplace is filled with innumerable franchise systems over a vast range of industries. We will look at giving anyone taking on the challenge and adventure that comes with opening a franchise business a step-by-step overview of the major stages along the way in this chapter. Please note the investment process has some variations from company to company, and timelines vary between systems.

Self-Evaluation: What appeals to you about opening a franchised business? Are you ready, willing and able to work long hours, including weekends and holidays (especially in the beginning)? Can you commit to following pre-determined business methods with very little variation, if any variation at all? Can you accept paying a portion of your profits to another entity (the franchisor)? Are you comfortable with the reputation of your business being largely dependent on the franchise's network and not just your business unit? Furthermore, how much of your personal cash are you willing to part with to establish the business? Unless you're fortunate enough to have enough money personally, do you have adequate assets (savings accounts, real estate, securities, etc.) to secure a loan?

Pick a Franchise Consultant to Assist You (Optional): Despite all of the information available online, it's still a good idea to enlist the help of a franchise consultant to help guide you through the process. Much like a real estate agent is a good ally in the purchase of a home, a franchise consultant has industry-specific knowledge and can relate possibly complicated topics (including aspects of agreements and disclosure documents) to you in a more understandable way. A franchise consultant could also potentially keep you from experiencing pitfalls that may happen without their expertise.

Research: What kind of businesses can your area sustain and are those the type of businesses you are interested in opening? Federal and state governments provide free access to statistics and other data. Plus, your common sense and gut feelings are good guides to figuring out what businesses are and could be sustainable in your locale. Use the info gathered to match up your personal situation and the business environment of your area with a suitable franchise system. Once you have narrowed your search down to a few strong contenders, request the franchise application from those companies. After the company decides that you could be a good match for their system, they will send you a copy of their Franchise Disclosure Document (FDD). The FDD will give an even deeper look into their business system.

Attend a 'Discovery Day': A discovery day is an in-depth meeting between the franchisor and one or more potential franchisees. It can take place at a local outlet, but most likely will happen at the company's corporate office. Often, the franchisee or franchisees in attendance will see presentations about what the franchisor can offer in terms of support, and can ask questions. If done at the corporate office, a tour of the different departments and introductions to franchisee training and support personnel are common.

Speak to Other Franchisees: Within the FDD provided by the franchisor is a listing of all current franchisees in their system. Find a few that are close to you and pay them a visit. Are they satisfied with the franchisor's support? Is the reality of the business in line with prior expectations (financially and otherwise)?

Find a Suitable Location: If you are located in a low traffic area or an area where there are no complementary businesses around, how are you going to get customers? The franchisor will use the FDD to delineate certain parameters for your territory. In addition, most franchisors assist with site selection. If you choose a suitable place for business on your own, the franchisor will have to approve your location before you can move forward.

Choose a Franchise and Secure Funding: After you have completed your research, it's time to make the big decision which franchise system will you invest in? Once you have decided, you will have all of the information necessary to complete a business plan and present it to potential lenders. There are numerous financing options out there for you to consider; bank loans, SBA (Small Business

Administration) loans, HELOC (Home Equity Line of Credit), etc. Remember, you will need enough cash reserves to cover expenses until the business begins to turn a profit, which in some cases can be months after opening.

Sign the Agreement: While many franchisors have rigid franchise agreements, some franchisors may be more flexible about negotiating terms in the agreement. If the franchisor is willing to negotiate certain terms (like lease parameters), it's a good idea to seek counsel from a lawyer with franchise-specific experience to find the best solutions for your particular situation. If the franchisor does have a rigid franchise agreement, that isn't a cause for concern. Remember, franchises are based upon a proven system and consistency of the brand. If the franchise agreement for the brand you chose is overly negotiable, it could be cause for deeper investigation.

Obtain All Necessary Permits and Insurance: Each industry has its own requirements for permits and insurance. Regulations by state, city, county, etc. will vary as well. The franchisor will likely have background knowledge of the permits and insurance needed to operate their business system; however, it's a good idea to check with local authorities to ensure compliance.

Hire Staff and Attend Training: The number of staff members needed to run the operation will depend on the type of franchise chosen. One of the most appealing aspects of franchising to those wanting to open a business is the training component.

Franchisors usually provide training in a combination of classroom and practical experiences to at least the franchisee and another manager. A copy of the franchise operations manual is also typically presented at this time.

Open Your Franchise Business: You will need to alert potential customers to their new marketplace option. Franchisors will often have defined processes for signage, ads, and other initiatives to be performed. Estimates for these initiatives will usually be a part of the start-up costs quoted in the FDD. Some franchisors will do a 'soft opening' before the 'grand opening'. A soft opening is designed to smooth out problems with the operation of the business before the big marketing blitz and hopefully larger crowds that will come with the grand opening. Some franchisors also arrange for a corporate trainer to be on hand at the franchise location during the opening days.

Chapter 21: Steps to Buying a Franchise

As mentioned in earlier chapters of this book a franchise is a way for an aspiring entrepreneur to start a business by following a proven model for success. The franchisee purchases a business unit from a franchisor and agrees to follow the established operating procedures in exchange for assistance in areas that include financing, marketing and staffing.

1. Determine the type of franchise

You should first determine the type of franchise that is right for you. This requires you to evaluate such things as the kinds of skills you already possess, the type of work environment you want to work in and how much "hands-on" involvement you want to have in the operation. You should also assess your goals, like how long you want to be in business and how much money you want to make.

2. Seek financing

Although franchisors can often help as far as arranging financing, you will still likely need to qualify for financing on your own. In general, you will need a personal credit score of 700 or better to secure financing. Possible financing sources include traditional bank loans, and you could also qualify for a government grant.

3. Obtain information

Begin to evaluate franchise companies that fit the profile of the type of franchise you are looking for. Contact the franchises you are interested in to have them send you preliminary information about the franchise and the steps involved in purchasing a unit.

4. Evaluate possibilities

Evaluate the franchises you're interested in by examining their Financial Disclosure Statement (FDD) provided by the franchisor, which gives you information on the franchise history and financial stability. You should also contact existing franchise operators to determine the pros and cons of operating a unit. If possible, spend some time at a franchise unit observing its daily operation.

5. Examine Franchise Agreement

The franchise agreement is the written document that spells out the obligations of the franchisor and franchisee. Elements to consider include the amount of royalties and fees you will have to pay the franchisor, the territorial rights you will have as far as the proximity of other units and where you can expand, and what assistance the franchisor is required to provide. Be sure to have the agreement examined by an attorney familiar with franchise law before you sign.

Having selected a franchise you wish to buy, there are a number of matters to which you have to attend before you can open for business. The following general guide should help you to complete the transaction more efficiently, both in terms of costs and also in terms of your time and effort.

Obtain as much detail from the franchisor as possible. Where the franchisor provides financial illustrations, study these carefully to satisfy yourself that the income shown in those illustrations satisfies your needs and requirements but always bear in mind that these are only illustrations and may be optimistic.

Whilst reviewing the information supplied by the franchisor, contact your bank manager (if you think you will need a loan) and discuss with him/her whether, in principle, the bank will lend you the money you require for the type of franchise you are contemplating buying. Most banks now operate fairly sophisticated information systems whereby bank managers have access to a central office from which they can obtain detailed information about many franchises, which will enable them to make a decision.

If your efforts above prove to be satisfactory; your next step is to arrange for a franchise lawyer to review the franchise agreement and advise you on it.

If you and your franchise lawyer are satisfied with the agreement see your accountant for advice as to the detailed financial aspects of the franchise. By this time you should have some idea of the sort of premises you will be occupying or your "territory" i.e. your area of operations in the case of a mobile franchise. The franchisor may have produced some financial projections for your particular business, if not, your accountant will help you to put together profit projections etc. and, if necessary, a business plan in support of your loan application with your bank.

At this stage you will probably be asked to sign the franchise agreement. You should be guided by your franchise lawyer as to the timing of signing the franchise agreement, which should be conditional on your securing satisfactory premises and a bank loan.

Where retail premises are involved, at this stage serious effort should be made to secure satisfactory premises and you should start talking to your franchisor about the details of converting the premises into a franchised outlet.

By this time your bank should have responded to your application for a loan and if the answer is yes you will be in a position to push those involved into finalising the lease for the premises. It is important that you do not enter into a binding commitment to take on premises unless and until you have your bank's agreement to the loan and you have signed the franchise agreement.

Once you have completed the acquisition of the premises you can go about converting the premises into a franchised outlet and going on the franchisor's training course.

The important thing to remember is that there will come a time when you have to make 3 significant commitments to 3 different parties

1. To the franchisor by signing a franchise agreement or an agreement to purchase a franchise.

2. To your landlord by signing a lease or an agreement to take a lease of the premises (or in the case of a mobile franchise, signing a lease, hire purchase or purchase agreement for a vehicle).

3. To the bank to take up the loan. Wherever possible you should aim to synchronise these different transactions so that you undertake the three commitments simultaneously.

Chapter 22: Talk to Existing Franchisees

It is vital when doing your research that you speak to existing franchisees in the network; they will be your most useful source of information and franchise advice. A good franchisor will always give you access to any of their franchisees.

If they are reluctant for you to do this, or only give you several names to contact, then they probably have something to hide and you can bet that the names they give you will be of their best achieving franchisees.

Franchisees have been there and done it, and so will tell you as it is. It is good to speak to those who are successful and also any that are not doing as well. If it is a good franchise then you will be able to identify why franchisees may not be doing as well, which will usually be down to personal circumstances. If however a pattern starts to emerge and a lot of franchisees are giving the same reason for their poor performance, then alarm bells should start ringing.

You can also ask to shadow a franchisee for a day. This will allow you to see what a typical day in the life of that franchisee is like, allowing you to see if it is something you would be interested in. The franchisor should be able to arrange this for you.

Franchisors may also allow you to speak to any franchisees that have left the network to give you an idea as to why they left. Again from this you should be able to get a better idea of how good the franchise is.

Potential questions to ask when buying a franchise business can include:

1. What was your reason for choosing this franchise? And what USP's does it have over its' competitors?

2. Where you happy with the support you got at the launch of your franchise? What support did you receive?

3. In your first year of trading was the support sufficient?

4. Have any problems occurred for you? If so, how did the franchisor deal with these? Overall is the franchisor supportive and available if you need advice?

5. How does the franchisor manage change in the business? How do they implement change? Is sufficient training and support given?

6. Does the franchisor visit you often? Is the operations manual and other supporting support documents well written, comprehensive and easy to follow?

7. Does the franchisor welcome feedback and ideas from franchisees? Have any ideas been implemented? Do franchisees have any say in the running of the business?

8. How does the franchisor market the business? What marketing do you specifically receive? Is it sufficient?

9. What are your sales figures like in comparison to the company as a whole? What is the company's weekly, monthly and annual sales figure typically like?

10. Are your ongoing fees reasonable? Is what you receive in return sufficient?

11. How much did you pay for the business? How much working capital did you require? Have you had a return on your money yet? If not, when do you forecast you will?

12. Are you allowed to buy multiple territories once you have built up your first franchise?

13. If you were taken ill and couldn't work, what help would the franchisor provide?

14. What changes have you seen in the business since you have been there? Have these been positive changes?

15. If you could change anything about the business, what would it be?

16. Would you do it all over again if you had the opportunity?

This is not an exhaustive list of questions to ask when buying a franchise, but it gives you a good start to what you should be asking the franchisee. Other questions may arise depending on what they answer.

The answers will help you build a picture of the franchise and at the end of it you should be in position where you either want to continue with applying for this franchise opportunity or have decided to look elsewhere.

Chapter 23: Advantages of Franchising

The question we get asked a lot is if it is good to buy a franchise?

In this chapter we will cover the advantages of franchising and create an argument for reasons to buy a franchise. The greatest franchise advantage to a franchise owner is that it reduces risk of business failure; because an ethical franchisor will have tried, tested and proven the business concept in the market place, most of the wrinkles will have been ironed out and the risks to the franchisee minimised. It is a well known fact that less than 7% of franchise owners fail within the first 3 years, as compared to over 90% of new business start ups.

Franchising enables a small businessman to compete with a big business. Through franchising a franchisee can take advantage of the economies of scale. All franchisees acting together can buy more cheaply and on better terms than an individual small business. Add to this the franchisor's support and the franchisee should have a distinct advantage over any independent small business competitor. It also enables a franchisee to trade under a recognised brand.

In theory at least, the products, equipment and system will have been previously market tested and therefore they come to the franchisee with a certain degree of ready acceptance by the consumer.

Through training imparted by the franchisor the franchisee climbs a very steep learning curve in short order, thereby increasing his chances of succeeding considerably. For example, someone who wishes to set up a dress hire business would find it very difficult to get the stock mix right at the outset. A franchisee, however, should have the benefit of his/her franchisor's experience who will be able to advise him/her on exactly the range and mix of the stock to carry, so many size 12 dresses, so many size 14 dresses etc.

No previous experience in a particular business is necessary for a franchisee to operate it. All deficiencies of know-how are made good, again, by training imparted by the franchisor. Indeed, one of the proudest boasts of franchisors is that they have the ability to turn a butcher, baker or candlestick maker into a fryer of chicken, dry cleaner or quick print shop operator. Any lack of knowledge on how to run a business is not a problem as a franchisor will provide the necessary training to the franchisee.

Thus, franchisees "hit the ground running" when they open a franchised outlet as they enter the market with a recognised brand name, proven business system and products and or services which have been market tested.

A franchisee has the ostensible backing of a large organisation and this is achieved by the pooling of resources, particularly in the field of advertising, marketing and promotions where each franchisee, by contributing a little, can have the benefit of a large fund for this purpose. Franchisees are therefore able to have their goods and services promoted through media which would otherwise be closed to them. In a well-run and structured franchise business, the franchisee is left to concentrate on selling the goods or services while at the same time receiving the benefit of continuous market research and development to improve the business and the franchised system.

In many cases franchisees are given exclusive territorial rights and this, in effect, gives them a monopoly over the area allocated to them, certainly in terms of doing business under the franchisor's trade name.

The franchisee has the benefit of the management and administrative experience of the franchisor in addition to which most franchisors provide back up and support including trouble shooting services to assist franchisees in their daily endeavours. This support includes managerial and administrative services, product information and marketing support.

Chapter 24: Disadvantages of Franchising

Advantages and disadvantages of franchising are both a reality. It is important that you give them full consideration before you start to think of buying a franchise. Compare both advantages and disadvantages and discuss any opportunity with an expert. This could help identify any issues which may not be obvious to someone new to franchising. The drawbacks fall into three categories.

1. Lack of independence.
2. Inflexibility.
3. Risk associated with the franchisors performance.

1. Lack of independence

An important feature of franchising is that every aspect of the business format is defined and each outlet is operated strictly in agreement with this format. Not everyone would be happy to operate a business under such constraints and you must consider how well you can accept this aspect of the franchising system when looking for a franchise to buy.

Discipline: Buying (licensing) a franchise means working within a system in which there is little freedom or scope to be creative. Almost every aspect of operating the business is laid down in the manuals.

Franchisor Monitoring: Regular field staff monitoring visits are welcome initially, but as time passes you will feel able to do your own trouble-shooting and you may come to regard the franchisors interest as an intrusion; it is after all your business.

Service Charges: At first these services are necessary and franchisees do not mind paying for them; however as time goes on, if less use is made of the franchisors services then franchisees can resent making the continuing payments.

Reputation: Each franchisee affects the reputation of the whole system depending on their performance and ability. In many franchises there is a wide gulf in the quality of product or service between the best and the worst franchisees. Thus any franchisee can harm the reputation of all outlets in the chain, even internationally.

2. Inflexibility

Responding to the market: Franchising tends to be an inflexible method of doing business as each franchisee is bound by the franchise contract to operate the business format in a certain way. This can make it difficult for a franchisor to introduce changes to the business format, refit outlets, or introduce new types of equipment. In some franchises it can be difficult for a franchisee to respond to new competition or to a change in the local market.

The job itself: What may seem an attractive challenge now could become boring after a few years so it is important that you choose a franchise to buy in which you will enjoy the work, or which has potential for growth.

3. Risk associated with franchisor performance

It is important to recognise that not all franchise businesses are soundly based or well run. In signing the franchise agreement you are formally binding yourself to a particular franchisor and it is therefore vital to select one which is competent and ethical. There are 4 different categories of franchisor:

a)   The Established Franchisor.
b)   The New Franchisor.
c)   The Unethical Franchisor.
d)   The Incompetent Franchisor.

Some should be avoided at all costs others will vary in attractiveness according to the level of risk you are prepared to take.

a) The Established franchisor: This represents the least risky type of franchise opportunity. The business format will have been fully tested in a number of locations, most likely abroad too, and although the initial cost of opening such a franchise may be relatively high, a franchise with this type of company will be highly attractive to anyone for whom security is important.

b) The new franchisor: There is nothing intrinsically wrong with a new franchise but great care must be taken in deciding to invest in any particular franchise. As franchisors incur high initial costs, they need a minimum number of franchises to break even. When a franchisor has fewer than the break-even number of franchises it is likely that.

   i.   More effort will go into selling franchises than into providing support services.
   ii.   There will be some deficiencies in services in order to keep costs down.
   iii. Financial resources will be strained.

In this start-up phase the franchisor is vulnerable to financial problems if franchises cannot be sold quickly enough. Franchises in this take-off phase are potentially those, which will earn the highest returns, for example if the product or service is outstanding in some way a large territory can be covered. With a franchisor you are in a position near that of an independent business greater return. Depending on the risks you are prepared to take, this type of franchise may be attractive, or one to be avoided.

c) The Unethical Franchisor: Unfortunately some franchisors have no intention of entering a long-term support relationship with the franchisee, instead they have heard that franchising is a way to make money quickly out of gullible franchisees. This is done by setting up a shell franchise; lots on offer but nothing to back it up, then selling such franchises to those who are so keen to become a franchisee that they fail to make a thorough appraisal of the business on offer. Make sure that you spot this type of franchise, take time to investigate different opportunities. You cannot afford to learn from your mistakes.

d) The Incompetent franchisor: These are franchisors who are not offering franchises to perpetrate fraud but who are incompetent in one or more of the following ways.

   i.   The basic business is unsound.

   ii.   The franchisor is under-resourced and may not be able to fund the initial running of the business.

  iii.   The franchisor has not run a pilot test so cannot confirm that the business is actually franchiseable.

  iv.   They have not used experience or accredited franchise consultants or lawyers.

   v.   Their manuals and start-up assistance and support is of poor quality.

Chapter 25: Why Franchise Fail

Despite franchising being a safer way of doing business, it does not mean that it is risk free. Many franchises have failed in the past and many will do so in the future. There are many reasons why this can happen and so it is vital that you undertake as much research as possible when looking to buy a franchise business in order to find the right franchise for you and to help you spot a bad franchise from a good franchise.

Below are some of the reasons why franchises can fail.

1. Lack off/no systems in the business.

Franchising is all about systems; being able to replicate systems is what makes a business franchiseable. An ethical franchise has everything documented and systemized so that it can easily be passed on to others to copy. If a business has no systems and instead relies solely on the skills of the individuals within the business, then it should not be franchised.

Some businesses however will ignore this and start to franchise their business anyway. These companies are usually only interested in making money fast. Once they sell the franchise to someone who doesn't have the required skills, then it fails as there is no systems for the franchisee to follow. A good franchise can usually take someone with no skills or experience in their business and train them to run a successful business by following their systems.

2. No track record.

A business can only be franchised if it has a track record. We are amazed at the amount of people who tell us that they have an idea for a franchise but don't actually have a business! The business comes first; it is not conceived at the same time as the franchise.

Those usually wishing to start a franchise without having a business are people who are looking to make money fast and think franchising can help them do that. Unfortunately sometimes these people convince others that it is a franchise resulting in them buying into it. This is why it is important that you know all there is to know about franchising and how to spot a bad franchise from a good franchise. Make sure that the franchisor has an established track record of running a business foremost and then their track record in franchising. They may be new to franchising but if they have been running a successful business then there is no reason why they can't also run a successful franchise if their business is franchiseable.

3. Location, location, location.

This saying is not just associated with buying a house, but it is also essential when buying a franchise. Half of the battle of a successful franchise is finding the right location for your business. Not all franchisees need to be in a city centre location or in a shopping mall, it depends on the nature of your business, but if you wanting to buy a food franchise that relies on footfall then you need to find a prime location for it. A good franchisor will spend time finding the right location for you.

4. Lack of marketing

Good franchisors will spend money on promoting the brand nationally as well as locally. Smaller and newer franchises with less brand awareness will require additional marketing and so the franchisor should have a detailed marketing plan in place. Ask the franchisor about their marketing activities and what they do to gain recognition and awareness. If the franchisor does not have a marketing plan then this could be worrying as how else will they create awareness to the brand.

A good franchisor will contribute some of the money they get from selling a franchise to a marketing fund to be used on local as well as national marketing. A franchisor that is just out to make money and not concerned about the business long-term will not be willing to put money towards marketing.

5. Competition

Check out what the competition is for the franchise in your local market. If there is no competition then there may not be a demand for the product, resulting in it not having much future market potential. Look into why there is no direct competition. Also check if the franchise is operating in any areas with similar demographics to your own, if so, is it successful?

If there is a lot of competition then you may have a problem gaining a share of the market. You have to look at if the franchise has any USPs that gives it a competitive advantage. If your product/service is inferior to what your competitors are offering then you may struggle in the market. Again look at markets similar to yours in which the franchise is operating to see how well it is doing.

6. Insufficient funds

One of the biggest reasons franchises fail is the franchisee under-estimating how much it is to buy a franchise and also run a franchise, as it is not just about having the money for the investment, but what about the costs you are going to incur when running the business? How do you pay staff salaries? How do you buy supplies? If your franchise business is not making money initially, you need to make sure you have enough money for the day to day operating costs. At the same time you need to also be able to pay your own bills and feed your family. Over-estimating what you need is the best way of approaching calculating how much money you will need to cover the cost to buy a franchise and run it successfully.

Chapter 26: Franchise Recruitment and Motivation

It is said the success of a franchise is a result of having good franchisees. It can equally be said that a franchisee's success can be attributed to their staff.

A franchisee needs to make their staff feel wanted and respected. If they feel like part of the family then they are more likely to work hard and stay with the business.

A company that offers no incentives and has a lack of moral in the workplace can expect a high turnover of staff.

Franchisees will work with their franchisor to make a plan for who they should be recruiting, what training to offer and how to motivate. They will put together a comprehensive training plan.

If the franchisor ensures that there is consistency throughout their network when it comes to recruiting and retaining staff, then they will become known as "a company to work for". If they can get this status, then it will be a lot easier for them to hire the best people.

Franchisees need to make sure that the people they bring in to the franchise, fits in with the culture of the business. If someone doesn't fit in then it can disrupt the workplace.

It is vital that the franchisee knows that they are looking for the skills and personality sought after. A good interviewer will know how to abstract the information they need from the interviewees.

Find out more about the interviewee. What are they looking for from the job, what are their aims and objectives, where do they see themselves in 5 years time? Their goals and aspirations need to fit with what you are offering. Also ask behavioural questions to help determine what a person would do in certain situation.

Staff motivation

Finding the right staff is not the hardest part of a successful work place, retaining staff is. It can be difficult to hold on to good people if not treated right. You need to use incentives to keep them interested. Monetary incentives are useful in the short term, but it is instead incentives that make employees recognise that the company is investing in their future that works e.g. training them in new skills, sending them on management training programs etc.

The culture of the business can help to retain staff. If franchisees can build a culture that shows that they are hands-on in the business and that they care and are willing to invest in the future of their employees and the business, then they are more likely to retain happy staff.

Franchisees sharing information such as weekly sales, new developments in the franchise network etc. can help staff members feel like an integral part of the company.

Simple incentives like bonuses for meeting targets, employee of the month, team building events etc can make a difference to a company.

Chapter 27: How to Avoid Franchise Scams

In the United Kingdom (UK) there are hundreds of businesses that call themselves franchises; however, despite promoting themselves as one, they are not all technically franchises.

With this in mind you need to know what to look out for when considering buying a franchise; how to spot a good franchise from a bad franchise. In this chapter we look at areas you should focus on and questions to ask before buying a franchise.

A good starting point would be to look at only those opportunities who are accredited by the British Franchise Association (BFA); this is the body that represents franchising in the UK; however, even if the franchise is a member of the BFA, you still need to do your homework and take as much franchise advice as possible, as being a member does not automatically guarantee success nor does it mean the franchise business won't fail.

Talk to the franchisor, a good franchisor will be happy to tell all and give you a good insight into their business. They will tell you about their ups and downs, challenges faced and overcome and will be happy to disclose any mistakes/failures they have made in the past. A good franchise will have used a trial period to identify these errors and would have worked hard to overcome them; however, be wary if someone tells you that their franchise is perfect and they have done no wrong, this is very rare.

You should equally have alarm bells ringing if they tell you that they can make you rich over night. This will never happen. An ethical franchisor will not make promises to earnings but may give you predictions based on other franchisees in the network; consequently managing your expectations.

Never be rushed into buying a franchise. If someone is constantly harassing you to make a decision then simply walk away. Finding the right franchise to buy is a massive decision as well as a massive investment. You need to do a lot of due diligence which any good franchisor would understand and recommend. They would be happy to give you all the time in the world you need to make the right decision for you and for them. If someone is pushing you into a decision and not open to talking about the company, it is more likely than not that they will have something to hide.

A franchisor should also be able to answer any questions you throw at them about their business. Make sure you have a prepared list of questions to ask when buying into a franchise. The franchisor should know the business inside and out and so should not falter at any questions you ask. If they cannot answer immediately, then they should be looking to get back to you as soon as possible.

Also be suspicious of any special promotions a franchise is running. A good franchise's track record would speak for itself; they wouldn't need any fancy gimmicks to sell their franchise. You can be sure that the cost of any freebies you think you are getting will be added on somewhere else in the package. Or there is a reason it is free.

Every franchise is new at some point, even McDonalds started off as a one unit franchise, and so you shouldn't be put off if a company is new to franchising. You should be aware though that the risks will be higher when buying a new franchise as it is less established. Check the history of the company itself; this should give an indication to the type of business it is. If the business is new then they shouldn't be franchising; you cannot make a franchise successful if the business has not proven that it can be successful. Only established, thriving businesses with a proven track record in their market should look at franchising. You need to therefore also avoid any "franchises" that have no company owned outlets as this is a franchise scam.

Make sure that what the franchisor is asking for in fees is worthy of what they offer you in return. The more established a franchise is, the more they will ask for as they will be able to give more back in return, i.e. public acceptance, market awareness, dominant position in market etc. Watch out for those who ask for a high investment but offer nothing in return, i.e. no track record in their industry, as they are just looking to make a lot of money fast.

The franchisee fee you pay should also cover support. Make sure that the franchisor has a dedicated and complete support system. If the support is limited or non-existent then this is something to be concerned about.

It is worthwhile seeking money advice and planning advice from your accountant to make sure that you can afford the franchise and have sufficient funds to cover the actual cost of running the franchise. Sometimes you may think you know the actual cost to buy a franchise but does it include the ongoing fees, working capital etc. Your accountant should be able to help with this, also ask the franchisor out right, how much does it cost to buy a franchise from you.

A good franchisor will provide you with a full list of all their franchisees that you can speak with, not just one or two they have selected, who you can be assured will be the best performing franchisees in the network and may not tend to be a true representation of the system as a whole. You should be offered the top and bottom performers to speak to. Also ask how many have left the system and if you can speak to them.

We cannot stress enough how important it is that you do your due diligence and take the right franchise advice (money advice from your accountant and franchise legal advice from an experienced franchise solicitor) so that you are 100% certain that it is the right franchise for you, and one that is reputable, before looking to buy it. If you are in any way in doubt about the franchise opportunity, then there is probably a good reason for this so maybe best to walk away.

Chapter 28: How to Get a Franchise Loan

Given that you are buying into a proven system for business success when you buy a franchise, it is hardly surprising that you have to make a fairly substantial investment.

But the good news is that because franchising is recognised as a safer route into business than simply setting up on your own, many banks are happy to lend you a substantial percentage of the initial investment provided you have been accepted by a reputable franchisor.

The typical arrangement is that you have to find one-third of the total start-up funds yourself; many people use savings or redundancy payments and the bank will lend you the other two-thirds as a business loan. Franchise funding is very competitive, however, and in some cases they will only lend half.

Most of the high street banks have special sections that deal with franchising which is a useful source of free advice. They provide information packs about franchising and financing and can help if you want to borrow money. Bank staff know about franchising, who the reputable and successful franchisors are and what level of risk they are taking.

So it may be worth talking to them before you even sign up for a franchise; banks often have stands at franchise exhibitions so you can compare what they have to offer.

Many franchisors have ongoing relationships with several banks that will look favourably on franchisees approved by the franchisor. So your franchisor may well suggest you talk to a particular bank or banks; though there is never a guarantee that you will be lent money.

When you apply for your business loan, franchise business plans are a must have. In most cases, you can count on your franchisor to help you draw this up, as it has done many time before. Some are frightened by this stage, but drafting a sound business plan is not a formality. Not only is it crucial to the long-term success of your business, but your franchise business loan broker will be looking to see that you fully understand the plan yourself rather than just repeating it parrot-fashion.

Also remember that you do not have to use your usual bank to obtain a business loan. Franchise businesses can pay to shop around to find a bank that understands your particular franchise well and where you get on well with the franchise business loan brokers.

Finally, just because you can raise money by borrowing does not mean that you should. The bigger your franchise loan, the more money your business has to make to meet the monthly repayments. If you have one or two bad months you could be under pressure and don't forget that if the franchise is set to become your major source of income it will have to generate enough profit not only to pay its own bills but your household expenses too.

Most banks have special sections that deal with franchising.

Chapter 29: The Importance of Ethical Franchising

According to a 2014 Franchise Business Economic Outlook report over 900,000 franchise establishments employ over 9.5 million people and generate over $850 billion in direct economic output in the U.S. alone and over 900 franchises operating in the UK; due to high number of franchise business, it can be hard to know which franchise is right for you.

The three largest macro business segments in franchising (by economic output) are.

1. Quick Service Restaurants (featuring carry-out or delivery service with limited in-restaurant seating).

2. Business Services (printing and packaging services, administrative services, employment/payroll services, tax preparation, accounting, IT services, etc.).

3. Personal Services (health care, education, entertainment/recreation, etc.).

Discover how to find a worthy investment as a franchisee...

With time, emotion and capital all being invested at sometimes substantial levels, it is crucial for potential franchisees to choose wisely when it comes to finding the right franchise to join.

A significant aspect of a franchisee's decision-making must involve the way the franchisor operates their business. It's commonplace to refer to franchisors that are operating the right way, and therefore worthy investments for franchisees, as adhering to the principles of 'ethical franchising'.

There are four key elements of an ethical franchise.

1. The business needs to be proven to work; not just the idea on paper or in someone's head with evidence that the product or service is saleable, and at a level of profit that will sustain both franchisees and franchisor.

2. It needs to be transferable and teachable, which means it can be run in multiple locations by multiple independent operators using the same system, brand and quality standards.

3. The franchise is structured and operated in accordance with the principles set out in the Code of Ethics for Franchising, which broadly covers advertising, recruiting and interactions with franchisees. The legally-binding franchise agreement, while weighted towards the franchisor to protect the brand and wider network, must be fair to both parties and comply with US law, UK law, European Community law and the European Code of Ethics.

4. All information on the business that is material to the franchise proposition and contract is disclosed without ambiguity to prospective franchisees and any

financial projections and earnings forecasts shall be objective and realistically achievable.

Ethics in practice

Now that you understand the principles behind a good franchise business, one which is worthy of consideration for your efforts and capital, it's worth discussing what ethical franchising means in reality. Broadly speaking, these are some of the telltale signs every potential franchisee should look out for in their franchisor.

1. Proven success

An established franchise should have existing franchisees that are successfully trading under the system; a new franchise should have at least conducted a pilot operation for a minimum of 12 months before recruiting franchisees; no pilot means no proof that the concept works.

2. Open disclosure

Good franchisors understand the benefits of having well-informed prospects. As well as a thorough understanding of daily operations, potential franchisees should ask any questions they have in order that they understand the franchise's ethos, sustainability, fees and proposition. Ask for proof that the business can be profitable for a franchisee, and find out what projections are based on; find out about the health and history of the network and the people behind the brand.

3. Legal considerations

It's perfectly normal for potential franchisees to have to sign a confidentiality or non-disclosure agreement before delving deep into the opportunity on offer; the payment of a deposit is commonplace too. But make sure that it is a refundable deposit, less any realistic tangible costs incurred and every franchisee should have (and take) the time and opportunity to have their franchise agreement reviewed by a lawyer: do NOT skip this step!

4. Initial training

Franchising is set up in most cases to allow someone to operate a business in a field in which they have no professional background. There should be sufficient training in place before a new franchisee begins trading to successfully launch; it might be on sales and marketing, administering the business, the systems, technical training but it must be in place.

5. Ongoing support

Training should not end once the franchisee begins trading. Continuing support should be on hand to the franchisee at scheduled intervals and on an ad hoc basis as required. It's what your monthly management service fees (MSF, or royalties) entitle you to, amongst other things. Find out what your franchisor is committed to providing.

6. Synergy

A franchise must NOT be dependent on selling and re-selling franchises to survive, it should be reliant on the long-term success of its franchisees to make its own profit through MSF. In fact, a good franchisor makes very little or no profit off the initial joining fees, which will mostly cover training costs and admin; that way, it's encouraged to help its franchisees do well. Ask for a breakdown of the start-up costs, which can vary widely; find out where your money is going, a good franchisor will tell you.

Chapter 30: The Franchise Agreement

In order to become a franchisee you will have to enter into a legal agreement with the franchisor, known as the franchise agreement.

What is the Franchise Agreement?

A franchise agreement should achieve three fundamental objectives.

1. Given the absence of specific franchise legislation, it should contractually bind the franchisor and the franchisee and accurately reflect the terms agreed upon.

2. It should seek to protect and benefit both the franchisor and the franchisee and the franchisors intellectual property.

3. It should clearly set out the rules to be observed by the parties.

The Terms

As there is no specific legislation or regulation for franchising, the franchise agreement becomes all-important in determining the rights and obligations of the franchisor and the franchisee and the relationship between them. In this respect the franchise agreement can be said to form the 'engine room' of the whole transaction. If difficulties should arise between the franchisor and the franchisee they will need to turn to the contract to see what, if any, rights and obligations have been provided in the franchise agreement.

What should one look for in a franchise agreement?

A franchisee will look for promises.

1. To train the franchisee and his staff.

2. To supply goods and or services.

3. To be responsible for advertising, marketing and promotions.

4. To assist the franchisee to locate and acquire property and have it fitted out and converted into a franchised outlet. (Similar considerations apply with regard to the acquisition of vehicles, fitting them out, equipping the franchisee etc.)

5. To assist the franchisee to set up in business.

6. To improve, enhance and develop the business system.

7. To provide certain management and possibly accounting services.

Franchisors will be anxious to ensure that the franchise agreement clearly sets out the obligations of the franchisee.

A franchisor will wish to.

1. Monitor the performance of the franchisee.

2. Protect them from unfair competition.

3. Protect his intellectual property.

4. Impose obligations and restrictions on the franchisee with regard to the exercise of the rights granted by him to the franchisee.

The Intellectual Property

These are in the nature of:
1. Trade Name.
2. Goodwill.
3. Methods of Production.
4. Confidential Information and know-how.
5. Copyright.

Trade Marks and Service Marks

Unless the franchise agreement contains sufficient safeguards to protect the franchisors intellectual property rights, the franchisor may find that he/she is unable to prevent infringement of his/her rights by a third party or an ex-franchisee.

Franchisors should be aware that it is not only the interests of the franchisor that these rights be protected.

Franchisees are equally concerned to ensure that the franchisor had done everything that is reasonably possible for him to protect the intellectual property rights in question. Many franchisees purchase a particular franchise because of the high profile a franchise enjoys in the market place. In many cases, a franchisee has the choice of which franchise to purchase in the same market sector and one of the reasons why a franchisee will have chosen a particular franchise is because of its strong brand image. It follows therefore that the franchisee will be anxious to ensure that in the event of infringement, the franchisor has taken sufficient steps to safeguard his ownership in his intellectual property rights so that he can stop infringement and thereby protect the reputation of that brand name both for himself and for his franchise network.

If the contract is weak on this point, franchisees will not consider that particular franchise to be a sound investment proposition because the franchisor will be limited in what he can do to prevent a 'copy cat' operation from being set up in direct unfair competition with a franchisee.

Brand names and trademarks are becoming increasingly important to business; they can increase the asset value of a company and therefore need to be adequately protected. The franchise agreement should therefore not only grant relevant rights to the franchisee and reserve rights for the franchisor, but should also contain mechanisms necessary for protecting the franchisors intellectual rights from infringement.

The Rules

All franchisees should be treated as a family and, as such, there should be no room for favourites.

This means that the franchise agreement should be in a standard form with all prospective franchisees being offered the same terms with no special deals being done. If a franchise agreement is to be non-negotiable then it is important, from the franchisees point of view, that it is well balanced in terms of rights and obligations of the parties and takes into consideration the franchisees concerns also.

If you are serious about buying a franchise, it is imperative that you get your franchise legal advice from an experienced franchise lawyer.

Again, in the absence of legislation or regulation, which tells the franchisor and franchisee what to do and how to behave, and given that franchisors and franchisees perceive the franchise relationship to be a long term one, it is important that the contract spells out very clearly what is expected and of each party to the contract.

The franchise agreement should therefore clearly:
1. Specify in detail the duties and obligations both of the franchisor and of the franchisee.
2. State the grounds upon which the franchisor will seek to terminate the franchise agreement.
3. Deal with the payment of franchise fees and the timing of those payments.
4. Set out the consequences of such termination.

Franchisors should be aware that under English law if an ambiguity arises in a franchise agreement the courts will tend to interpret the ambiguity in favour of the franchisee. They reason that, as the draftsman of the contract, it is the franchisors responsibility to make sure that he/she gets it right and therefore they will not allow him/her to benefit from any ambiguity which may well arise as a result of unclear drafting.

Some thought has to be given to the franchisees and their objectives and provision should therefore be made in the franchise agreement to deal with what is to happen should the franchisee die or become permanently incapacitated .

It is also advisable to deal with the question of what is to happen if a franchisee wishes to sell his business during the term of his franchise agreement . Here, as in other matters, a balance has to be struck between the need of the franchisee to realise his/her investment as and when he/she wants to and the requirement of the franchisor to approve those coming into the franchise network and to prevent those leaving the network (for whatever reason) from continuing to use the franchisors trade secrets and competing unfairly.

The franchise transaction is complex and the franchise agreement must respect that complexity. Experience has shown that those franchisors who take the matter of the franchise contract lightly pay dearly for their mistake.

To the franchisee, the franchise contract represents an investment. His/her business depends upon it to the extent that his business may disappear should it terminate. For the franchisor, the franchise agreement is an income producing asset which will ultimately have a place on his/her balance sheet.

How to negotiate franchise agreement issues.

It's important to remember that buying a franchise isn't like going to a shop and purchasing some jeans; you won't be able to return it with a receipt and get a refund.

Being a franchisee means that you will be bound by a franchise agreement that is legally binding. If you don't like what you have signed, you will have to challenge it through the civil courts; a timely and costly process.

The best way to avoid future legal wranglings is to thoroughly prepare for the deal. As with any legally binding contract it's essential that you have the franchise agreement contract looked over by a lawyer who specialises in franchising.

Regardless of whether you are a legal expert it's also a good idea to look over the franchise agreement contract thoroughly yourself too. You are the one who will be responsible for the business, so it's important you thoroughly understand any issues raised in the contract.

Chapter 31: Franchise Operations Manual

The operations manual is a franchisee's best friend!

It outlines everything a franchisee needs to know about running their franchise business and executes the obligations outlined in the franchise agreement. It provides franchise guidelines for running a successful replicate of the franchisors business.

The operations manual provides the franchisee with support and guidance and helps the franchisee to meet the quality of standards expected of them by the franchisor. It also ensures consistency across the network which in turn helps the franchisor to protect their brand. Every franchisee in the network is therefore singing off the same hymn sheet.

In order for the franchisee to follow the manual accurately it needs to be detailed and informative. Each manual will depend on the nature of the business, e.g. franchises that are in the food industry will need to cover health and safety as well as food hygiene in their manual. Overall this franchise guide should generally cover the following:

About the company: Its' history, who runs the company, who the legal advisors are, the aims and objectives of the company.

Support: What support the franchisee will receive, who the support team are and how to go about getting the right support i.e. channels of communication.

Launch timetable: What needs to be done and by when, what the obligations of the company are to assist the franchisee in the opening of their new franchise.

Training: What training the franchisee will receive, who takes the training, what training qualifications the company has, what additional training the franchisee should expect to receive after the franchise has been launched, any national sales meetings the company runs.

Recruiting staff: What positions the franchisee needs to fill, what should be in the job description and what skills the applicants should posses.

Office policies: How to set up the office, customer service standards, process for dealing with complaints, employee dress code, managing visitors, computer usage and access policy.

Office maintenance: Housekeeping duties, daily procedure for opening and closing the business, the responsibilities of staff, office cleaning, office administration, health and safety and inventory maintenance.

Office equipment: What the franchisee is given, how to maintain it and list of approved suppliers for further purchases.

Administration: Record keeping, accounts and finance.

Reporting: The procedures the franchisee should use for reporting back to the franchisor, what happens if the report is not sent over and other records and reports need to be kept for audits and inspections.

Vehicle administration: Leasing of cars and the policy for dealing with auto crime.

Marketing: The requirements, who the target audience are and how best to target these audience using the most effective media channels.

Pricing: How you set prices and fee structures.

Sales: Managing leads and referrals, telephone selling procedure and sales presentations.

Insurance: What insurances are required, and what is covered within these policies, the suppliers to use and risk management and security.

Corporate structure: Setting up the franchise business, what the different types of structure and legal requirements.

Financing: Who the existing financing agreements are with, what alternative financing is available.

Company protection: Information on using copyrights, proprietary and trademarks, and how to avoid misuse.

Field operations: Looks at health and safety outside of the office and risk management.

Resale, transfer, renewal and closing of the business: Conditions for renewal, procedures for business transfer, termination of the business.

Expansion and relocation: What the procedures are if you wish to expand a new or an existing territory and also if you wish to relocate the business.

Chapter 32: Franchise Training

It is essential to evaluate what training you should expect to receive from the franchise you are interested in.

A good franchisor will invest heavily in training their franchisees so that they provide them with all the skills they need to make their franchise a success; a bad franchisor is only after your money.

The ethical franchisor will make sure that their franchisees and their staff are fully prepared in all aspects of operating the business before letting them open.

The training is uniform across the network so that all franchisees operate the business in the same way. This consistency helps to ensure long term success for both the franchisee and the franchisor.

The franchisor is responsible for ensuring that they provide training that is competitive and current.

Training can take the format of "classroom training" which usually happens at Head Office in a dedicated training room, and "hands-on" training where you are trained in either an actual franchise unit or an operating unit that has been built in Head Office and which mirrors that of an actual franchise outlet; hands-on allows you to grasp how everything physically works. Most franchisors will offer a combination of the two. The training will be undertaken by a skilled and qualified instructor who knows how the business operates inside and out and can take up to 8 weeks.

You will also have a training team with you during your first few weeks of trading to make sure that you remember everything the training taught you, and to offer their experience on running the franchise. This on-site training is invaluable.

If the company introduces change, new systems, products etc, the franchisor should make sure that the change does not disrupt the network and that all franchisees are comfortable with the change. To do this they will make sure that adequate training is given.

Your training should also have covered how to recruit and train staff. This is important if your franchise is a retail business where the nature of the work means that staff turnover can be high. You will need to be able to recruit and train staff effectively and efficiently.

The Franchise Agreement should outline the franchisor's obligation to the franchisee i.e. what they are committed to provide. Does it look sufficient? Does it look value for money?

To find out more about what the franchisor provides, ask them.
1. What areas of the business do you cover?
2. How long does the training last?
3. Who takes the training?

4. What is their experience?
5. Do they have qualifications?
6. What type of training do I get?
7. Classroom? Hands-on? Or both?
8. Do you provide a training manual for the franchisee to keep?
9. Do you train key staff members or just the franchisee?
10. Do you have a training team/person that is with the franchisee after the launch of the business?
11. Do you offer training if changes are implemented into the system?
12. Do you offer any advanced training programs?

Speak to existing franchisees and ask them.
1. What training did you receive?
2. Was it hands-on or classroom or both?
3. How long did it last?
4. Who took it?
5. Is large percentage of course about the business?
6. Anything they should include?
7. Did they train your staff or just you?
8. Did you receive any training manuals?
9. After you opened your business, what training did you receive in the first week?
10. Are you offered any additional training as the business progresses?
11. Have you had to be trained in anything new e.g. now systems, software, products etc?
12. Overall how do you rate the training provided?

13. What would you change if anything?

A good franchisor will be dedicated to providing uniformed, continuous, detailed and measured training.

Chapter 33: Franchise Support

Having established that the franchise is reputable, and it is a business you see yourself being part of, you then need to examine the strengths and weaknesses of their franchise operation.

You need to be comfortable that they will provide you with the required support you need at the launch of your franchise business and on an ongoing basis. This is central to the success of your franchise.

If you receive no or little support, your business will be on a downward spiral from the start. You will have no one to turn to when problems arise and will continue to make the same errors time after time. You will become demoralized and start to detest going into work each day.

A good franchise company will be available 24/7 to help you with any problems you have. They will be there throughout your launch and will continue to provide you with the dedicated support you need on an ongoing basis. They should provide you with a detailed operations manual that outlines all areas of running your business.

They will have support teams in place to deal with your queries and will regularly visit you at your workplace to make sure that you are coping and to make sure that the business is being run efficiently.

You should also ask the franchisor and franchisees about implementing change and what support you would receive e.g. new computer systems, rebranding, new product development etc.

How do they support your marketing activities? Who does what and what is provided?

Do they offer cover if you go on vacation? What happens if you are ill, what support do they provide?

What support would you receive to help you with staff recruitment and training? Do they train your staff for you or train you to train your staff? Or do they not offer any training support?

Good franchisors will hold an annual conference where franchisees can get together to discuss any issues or ideas they have, and to hear from the franchisor on their plans to take the business forward.

The franchisor should also assist with making sure that you have the correct insurance for your business as well as any certificates and accreditations you may require e.g. health and safety.

Ask other franchisees what support they receive and what changes they would make. This is the best way to get an insight into the business. You need to be happy with the results of all your research before you should consider entering into an agreement with the franchisor.

Chapter 34: Marketing Your New Franchise

Of course, the biggest difference between the conservative and the aggressive growth franchisor is in the areas of franchise sales and marketing. While the conservative franchisor will be content to let prospective franchisees come to him and operate in a reactive fashion, the aggressive franchisor will want to "make it happen."

Brochures. Your marketing efforts start with the development of professionally designed materials. A full-sized, four-colour brochure is virtually the cost of entry in modern franchising. This brochure not only sells the franchise opportunity to the prospective franchisee; it also plays a key role in demonstrating the credibility of the franchise to key influencers; accountants, attorneys, bankers and spouses, who will play a key role in the franchise selection process. The design of a good brochure will cost between $7,000 and $10,000. Printing this brochure, depending on print process, paper quality, quantity printed, and a variety of design specifications (full bleeds on pages, dye cuts, stapling, etc.), will cost another $8,000 to $10,000.

For companies with physical units, or companies that plan on using a lot of direct mail or trade shows to promote their franchise, another great tool is the mini-brochure. This brochure, typically done in a two or three-fold format, can be produced in quantity relatively inexpensively (design costs and printing costs totalling around $5,000), and serves as a lead generator more than as a credibility piece.

Internet. A professionally designed website is also essential. In addition to franchise information, your website should be equipped with lead collection forms and, ideally, an auto-responder matrix that helps you sort the wheat from the chaff and this site needs to be optimized for franchising. While websites are increasingly less expensive to create, you should still budget $5,000 to $10,000 for a really good one.

For franchisors looking for more aggressive growth, franchise sales videos are increasingly important in the sales process, as streaming video becomes a more integral part of the internet. Professionally produced video promoting the franchise offering can generally be developed for between $5,000 and $10,000.

Marketing Budget. At least as important as the marketing materials will be your marketing budget. Depending on the size of the investment in a franchise opportunity, you should budget between $5,000 and $7,500 (and in some instances more) per franchise to be sold to a promotional budget. If you are planning to sell 20 franchises in your first year, an annual marketing budget of between $100,000 and $150,000 is not at all unrealistic. Of course, some of these funds will be recaptured as you begin to realize franchise fee income, but since it takes an average of 12 weeks to sell a franchise, as an aggressive franchisor, you should have at least five to six months worth of advertising money or about half your annual budget on hand when you get started.

To optimize these expenditures, you should also invest in primary market research (to better understand your prospective franchisee) and in a first-rate marketing plan. While inappropriate for more conservative franchisors, these planning activities will add another $10,000 to $15,000 to the budget.

Hiring a Sales Force

The single biggest investment you will have in the development of an aggressive franchise company will be in your people.

Most companies getting into franchising for the first time do so by leveraging off their existing staff. Often, the business founder acts as the primary franchise salesperson, with support from staff in the areas of operations and training and while this works in most growth scenarios, the more aggressive the growth scenario, the sooner you should plan on bringing on incremental staff to fill key roles in the areas of franchise sales, franchise training and field support.

The first hire for the aggressive franchisor is generally the franchise salesperson. A proven franchise salesperson will generally command a compensation package in the low six figures, with at least some of this package being performance based. Top franchise sales pros can command twice the salary or more but are generally worth their weight in gold. Again, you should expect the franchise salesperson to begin earning his keep by selling franchises relatively quickly (a good franchise salesperson should be able to sell 12 to 20 franchises per year), but you should anticipate the need to fund at least four to six months of their salary without any fee income. Add to this salary the fees you will pay to an executive recruiter to locate this top talent (who will generally command a fee of 25 percent of first year's compensation), and you can probably budget $75,000 in personnel costs before selling the first franchise, should you go this route.

Other hiring generally comes later after franchise sales have started and the royalty stream is established but again, the more aggressive the growth, the earlier these hires need to take place.

Cash Flow Analysis

The best way to get a reasonable understanding of franchise costs is to develop a cash flow analysis that accounts for all your hiring, marketing, legal and development needs, as well as for the inflow of franchise fees, royalties and other sources of income. While many factors will influence your ultimate cash need, a good rule of thumb is that an aggressive franchise program may require a cash flow budget of $250,000 to fund development costs and franchise growth until franchise sales begin "paying for" incremental personnel and advertising needs.

But remember, rules of thumb, like thumbs in a softball game, are often broken. Many franchisors have succeeded in growing significant franchise companies with far less while others have failed at franchising after investing far more.

While it is important to be properly capitalized to franchise, it is important to remember that the costs of creating this franchise company, even in aggressive growth scenarios, is often less than the cost of starting just one more company operation. That investment in a franchise program can grow to be a franchisor with hundreds, or perhaps thousands, of franchised units, providing you with leverage not found in any other means of business expansion.

Chapter 35: Legal Structure of a Franchise

Franchises just like any other business entity can be set-up with a number of business formats. Before you choose which format would be the most suitable for your particular franchise business, it's a good idea to ensure you understand the unique aspects of the franchise format itself.

1. Master franchisor

Some of the larger international franchises can have complex logistical set ups, but what you have to remember as the franchisee is that the person you buy your franchise license from may not be the overall owner of the franchise business. These are usually privately owned companies, but can in some instances be public companies as well. Many of the most successful franchises are based in the USA and Europe. The master franchisor is, therefore, the company that owns the intellectual property to the franchise format. Understanding the overall structure of the franchise business you are buying into commercially astute so you understand how you as franchisee fit into the overall company structure.

2. Franchisor

This is the person or organisation you as the franchisee have the closest relationship with. The franchisor will have the authority to sell the franchise format in their particular country or territory as set out by the master franchisor.

It is in the franchisor's interest to offer you as a potential franchisee all the information you need to make a decision to buy a new franchise branch. It's rare for a franchisee to have much contact with the master franchisor, as all communication goes through the regional franchisor. The franchisor will often be a privately owned company, but can also be a public company in some instances.

3. Franchisee

You are the franchisee in the franchise hierarchy. What kind of business format you choose will depend on the franchise itself as the market you are selling to can often determine the best type of business format to use. Sole traders, partnerships (limited and unlimited) and private companies (limited) are the traditional choices of business format for the actual legal structure of a new franchise.

4. Intellectual property

The most important component of a franchise is its intellectual property. The overall branding, business idea, unique process or whatever makes the franchise stand out from the other business to give it a unique selling point is the foundation of the franchise as a whole.

It's important to understand that as the franchisee you do not own any of the intellectual property in your franchise. This is ultimately owned by the master franchisor; however, because intellectual property law varies across the world, you may find that the master franchisor has a subsidiary in your country that they use to protect their intellectual property in your region.

You may have no legal right to the intellectual property in the franchise you buy, but you will be expected by the franchisor in your country to take all possible steps to protect the overall intellectual property of your franchise.

5. Franchise business structure

From a legal standpoint your lawyer will be able to give you advice on the best business format for the type of franchise you are running. For instance if your franchise is run part-time from your home, it's unlikely that you will need to form a limited company. But talk your options through with your legal advisors, as you may not have considered a business format that could have other advantages such as lowering your tax liabilities.

Chapter 36: How to Grow Your Franchise

There is a pattern to the development and growth of a franchise, although no two systems nor the problems to overcome will be identical. These are the basic, underlying challenges you should expect to encounter on the route to franchise success.

1. Finding a business idea

You may be running a business already like coffee shop, sign manufacturer, fast print, bookkeeping service; that you want to use as your business idea. Or you may decide to devise an idea from scratch by brainstorming, networking and researching a range of possible options.

2. Organising the first pilot operation

To build a franchise, you should consider devoting at least one year to piloting your basic business idea. This will enable you to test your strategies for sales, marketing, product or service delivery, pricing and staffing. Virtually every business start-up plan has to be changed during the first months of its implementation. High failure rate figures, particularly during the first 30 months after start-up, confirm this; however, if you have an established business which is doing well, you may decide to let this represent your pilot.

3. Establishing transferability

With the pilot in place, your next step will be to set up an identical outlet in a different location. This will test how easy it will be to find new premises, hire new staff, organise a launch and all the other aspects of transferring the skills and success of your original enterprise. It involves a steep learning curve, but there is no more certain test of your business idea's transferability.

4. Drawing up key documents

Before you can start looking for franchisees, you will need three essential documents.
a. Operating Manual: This puts on paper detailed instructions that will guide your franchisees in running their outlets.

b. Franchise Contract: This sets out the legal obligations of the franchisor and franchisee.

c. Franchise Prospectus: Your marketing tool for recruiting franchisees.

Expect to put a great deal of time and hard work into each of these. You may also need to pay for external help from management consultants, solicitors and accountants.

5. Arranging financial support

Setting up a franchise system is costly. You may have to invest over $100,000 in development costs to franchise even the least expensive systems, before reaching break-even point. Trying to finance system development purely from franchise sales and royalty fees seldom succeeds. When planning the financial side of your franchise, you could consider bank loans, investment by business partners, or family members in addition to your own funds.

6. Franchisee recruitment

The tried and tested methods of attracting the interest of potential franchisees are usually quite costly. But with no previous track record or brand awareness to draw upon, spending this money may be unavoidable. Expect to spend money on taking stands at franchise exhibitions and advertising in the national press. Expect to spend time filtering down the 40 or 50 leads that are typically required to yield a single franchisee.

7. Establishing management control and field support systems

As you gain franchisees, to ensure that the system runs smoothly you will need to reinforce your own management team in such areas as; franchisee training and support, advertising, setting up reliable supply lines, and collecting royalties.

8. Achieving break-even

The franchise process is heavily front loaded, in that you need to have in place a tried and tested business system, management team and fieldwork support well before a steady flow of money starts to come in from franchisee fees and royalties. For most systems you can expect break-even only after 4-5 years and with 30-40 outlets trading.

9. Communicating with your franchisees

As your franchise continues to grow, business systems will come to replace the personal communications that you used in the early days. For any business, two-way communications are essential; especially if you want to introduce changes. You may need to set up a formal franchisor-franchisee advisory committee, publish company newsletters and fact sheets, and hold national or regional conferences.

10. Surviving post-maturity

Your franchise will have reached 'maturity' when regular royalty fees are coming in from the franchisees. It may take five years to reach this point, but this will be no time to relax. You need to be constantly alert for competition in your chosen field, and to come up with improvements to your product or service that will help to keep you ahead. As your army of franchisees continues to grow, the scale of your management support systems should also grow. Here careful management is particularly important. If you expand your support systems too soon, you will have to carry high overheads. But if you do so too late, you risk undermining the confidence and goodwill of your franchisees.

Chapter 37: How to Succeed in Franchising

If you have just discovered franchising as a concept of self-employment and you are starting to look into the myriad of franchise options on offer, it can be tempting to blindly look through every website directory you can find.

But, before you do that, there are some simple steps that can put you in a much stronger position to thrive as a franchisee when you do take on your own business. Act in haste, repent at leisure? Not if you are on the ball from day one.

So before you spend hours trawling franchise sites, spend a few minutes reading these tips and put yourself firmly in a place to maximise your chances of success.

1. Honesty is the best policy.
This old adage should be at the forefront of every prospective franchisee's mind from the outset. It should encompass everything that informs your decision on which brand to invest in.

What we are talking about is honesty with yourself. There is plenty to consider, which is why you should be taking your time, not rushing, when buying a franchise and why looking inwards is the crucial first step in the process.

2. Your skill set.

Take time out to list what you bring to the table. Franchising revolves around transferrable skills; a good franchise offers substantial initial and ongoing training and support which is why the overwhelming majority of franchises are suitable to people with no direct prior professional experience in whatever industry the franchise is in.

So think about your top skills; sales, administration, business growth, getting hands-on in a business, marketing, people management, networking; what do you do best? Finding a business that plays to your strengths will immeasurably improve your chances of franchise success.

3. Your personality.

The type of person you are can be crucial to your business outlook. Are you outgoing or an introvert? Are you naturally adept at working with, and leading, teams, or better on your own? What are you passionate about? Looking honestly at your own traits can give you good insight into the type of operation you are likely to be successful with.

Combining your personality traits with your skill set can give you a powerful indicator of the franchise that is right for you.

4. Driving force.

First, think about what kind of operation you want to run, and why. Do you want to be hands-on, or a business manager and developer? Out on the road or working from home? Lone wolf or avid networker? Is potential profit the most important factor in your decision-making, or is a better family balance higher on your priorities?

Second, take time to understand what is driving you to want to become a business owner. Are you tired of working long hours for the reward of others, is it succession planning for your kids, to be a part of your local community, to have control of your own professional life, to take home more money; there are a plethora of reasons that bring people into franchising.

Knowing what your driving forces are is important in order to determine the franchise opportunity that can give you what you are looking for.

5. Finances.
To put it simply, work out which franchises you can afford. There is a huge range of franchises to suit almost every budget, from a few thousand up to hundreds of thousands, but before you fall in love with an idea it's important to know the ceiling of your liquid capital combined with any funding you can access.

Work out how much finance you personally have available (and are willing) to invest in the franchise, then consider your funding options which can add substantially to that figure. By far the most popular option is bank lending; banks like the franchise model because they can access historical data from already-trading franchisees with other sources including family and even franchisors, a few of which will finance the cost of starting up over a period of time for the right franchisee.

In the UK, British Franchise Association (bfa) member franchises are looked upon favourably by the major banks because they understand the strict criteria involved in gaining bfa membership; which includes proof of financial sustainability to support a network properly, and evidence of previous franchisee success. For franchisees of reputable franchisors, banks will typically lend up to 50-70 % of the start-up cost, depending on how long they have been trading. Of course, regardless of the brand you will still need a strong business plan to gain bank funding.

To give an example, if you have £20,000 in liquid capital to invest then with an established franchise in good standing with the banks you can potentially take on a business with a total start-up cost of approximately £65,000, around 70% bank funding on top of your £20,000. For a newer brand, it might be more like £40,000.

Doing the maths gives you a clear idea of the range of franchises that are realistic for you, financially speaking. You must also remember to consider working capital in the early days of the business before you are turning a profit.

6. Your circumstances.
Running a franchise is a serious proposition. You must take your personal life and the circumstances of those around you into consideration. Discussions

with your partner and family are crucial, you will need their support when you take the leap into self-employment and many franchisors will want to see that you have that support.

Think about what you want to get out of the business and how it might impact those around you. Some franchises, at least in the early days, require more than a 9-5 undertaking, while others are set up to appeal to parents and fit perfectly around a young family and the school run. Be prepared to keep up with the business demands and know that you can do so around your other commitments.

It's worth repeating time and again that buying a franchise is not a decision that should be rushed. It's a legal, financial and emotional commitment and one that could change your life for the better if you approach it the right way. A long, hard look in the mirror is a good first step!

Chapter 38: Building a Successful Franchise Marketing Strategy

Once you have completed your initial training as a new franchisee, you will be full of enthusiasm for the products and services you are about to offer. It's at this time that the reality dawns on you that you are required to master many skills and wear different hats, two of the most important of which will be marketing and sales. You may not feel confident or comfortable in this role, but it is one you will need to get good at, and quickly too.

Successful marketing is about accumulating knowledge and is an art as well as a science. But you shouldn't find the process daunting; embrace the task of keeping up with the changing demands of customers and finding new ways to get them through your doors or on the end of a phone.

Creating a long term goal

There are no hard-and-fast rules for creating a marketing strategy. It's up to you to set your own goals; however, as a general rule, you need to ask what you want your franchise to achieve in one year's, two years' or even five years' time compared to where it would be without a marketing strategy.

Depending on your past employment history, you may have previous sales and marketing experience, along with tactics that may or may not have worked well in the past. What all new franchisees bring to the table is the experience of being sold to, and this may substantially colour how you feel about being marketed to, and how you feel about being labelled as a salesperson.

What marketing strategy will already be in place for franchisees?

Many of the basics of marketing will already have been provided within the franchise system and structure you have chosen. This ensures that many of the common marketing challenges associated with stand-alone, independent businesses are removed. These include:

1. Where to advertise? Franchisors already have a format that works for you to follow.
2. How to use social media? Franchisors may have a central page on Facebook for the brand and an active Twitter account.
3. What makes the ideal customer? Franchisors have already profiled this for you.
4. What are the best price points? These have already been tested and refined.
5. Building a recognised brand. The franchisor has already spent time and money on this.

As well as assistance with the above your franchisor may have given you some training on tried and trusted sales techniques that they feel work effectively.

What are the marketing challenges for franchisees?

Nevertheless, as a new franchisee you are still likely to come up against a number of challenges including:

1. Painfully long selling cycles.
2. Bad sales habits eroding margins.
3. Prospects demanding and getting costly price concessions.
4. Being part of a bidding war.
5. Struggling to differentiate yourself in a competitive market.

Tips for your marketing plan

Regardless of the challenges, centralised marketing programmes are one of the greatest strengths of franchise programmes. The large central marketing fund will allow for spends, such as a TV campaign, that you may never be able to afford as an individual franchisee; however, in addition to the overall marketing spends, you will still need to market your individual business on a day-to-day basis, and prove that you can attract and retain customers and generate repeat sales.

Here are some tips to remember when devising your marketing plan.

1. Start by setting clear objectives; where do you want your franchise to go?
2. Set clear financial targets for these objectives.
3. Define your target market and identify your potential customers.
4. Understand the brand and the values you have bought into and need to communicate.
5. Plan your promotion strategy.
6. Set a budget.

7. Devise a schedule.

Measuring success

Once you have got your plan in place, it's a good idea to check your marketing and Public Relation ideas with your franchisor. It may be, for example, that local radio advertising has already been tried and found to be a very expensive mistake. Avoiding such pitfalls is one of the advantages of buying into a franchise.

With the general franchise marketing strategy in place, and your own marketing plans devised to complement it, your business should have a good grounding to find and understand new and existing customers, and, most importantly, drive sales.

Chapter 39: Franchise Frequently Used Words

Buying a franchise business, as like any business start-up, can be a complex process. To help simplify it for you we have listed below an extensive list of common franchise terms and their definitions.

Advertising Fee: It's a contribution made to an advertising fund that the franchisor manages for the franchise system. The franchisor customarily uses the fund for national advertising and marketing, or to attract new franchise owners, but not to target your particular outlet. It's usually less than three percent of the franchisee's annual sales and usually paid in addition to the royalty fee. Not all franchisors charge advertising fees.

Approved Supplier: Suppliers approved or chosen by a franchise company.

Area Franchisee/Area Developer: Buys the rights from the original franchisor to develop the system in a defined region. An area developer cannot sell franchises.

British Franchise Association (bfa): The bfa, since 1977, has established an ethical code of conduct for franchisors in the UK and ensures the strict enforcement of this code. Over 300 franchises are members of the bfa and adhere to this code of conduct.

Broker: These are independent professionals who market on behalf of franchisors, selling their franchisees on a fee-paying basis. Potential franchisees must always independently evaluate their chosen franchise.

Business Format Franchising: A license to operate a business using a franchisor's product, service and trademark under certain guidelines for a specified time.

Business Plan: A plan that outlines the objectives of a business and the steps necessary to achieve those objectives. This can include financial projections and the planned steps for expansion. If you are seeking funding from a bank or building society you will often be asked to provide your business plan to secure borrowing. In fact, many of the well-known banks can offer advice and assistance on formulating a comprehensive and achievable business plan for your franchise.

Company-Owned Outlet: An outlet operating under a franchise company brand, but that is owned by the franchisor as opposed to a franchisee. Company-owned outlets are often used by franchisors to try new ideas and systems before implementing them across the franchised outlets within the network.

Copyright: The franchisor produces manuals and other documentation to ensure the franchise system is uniform. These are the franchisor's documents and he/she has copyright over them.

Development Type: The Development type is the method by which the franchisor wishes to build their franchise network. See Unit Franchise, Multi-unit Franchise, Area Developer, Regional Franchisee and Master Franchise.

Distributorships: Manufacturers and wholesalers grant permission to businesses and individuals to sell their products. A distributorship is normally not a franchise; however, certain distributorship arrangements may qualify as a franchise, may be licensed or be adjudged a business opportunity requiring disclosure.

Earnings Claim: Is any information the franchisor gives to a prospective franchisee which allows you to attempt to predict a range or level of potential sales, costs, income, or profits.

Estimated Initial Investment: A detailed listing of all fees and expenses you can expect to incur in starting a franchise. This listing represents the total amount that you would need to pay or get financing for, including fees paid to the franchisor; estimates for furniture; fixtures and equipment; opening inventory; real estate costs; insurance inventory, etc. This estimate should include a provision for working capital through the start-up phase.

Exclusive Territory: As a franchisee you can, with the consent of the franchisor, be given an exclusive area around your operation. This area can be large or small and no other franchisee or company owned business would be allowed to operate there.

Franchise: The rights you acquire to offer specific products or services within a certain location for a declared period of time.

Franchise Agreement: Outlines the expectations and requirements of the franchisor and describes their commitment to the franchisee. The Franchise Agreement includes information that covers territorial rights of the franchisee, location requirements, training schedule, fees, general obligations of the franchisee, general obligations of the franchisor, etc.

Franchise Fee: An up-front entry fee, usually payable upon the signing of the contract (franchise agreement) for the right to use the franchisor's name, logo, and business system. Often the franchise fee is also the consideration paid for initial training, site selection, operations manuals, and other help given by the franchisor before the opening of the business.

Franchisee: The operator or owner of a franchise.

Franchise Resale: The process of buying a franchise that is already up and running. Franchisees sell on their franchise for a number of reasons; retirement, another business venture, moving overseas, have made their money etc. Whilst the investment may be higher than buying a new franchise, buying a franchise resale minimises the risk of failure and is operational from day one.

Franchise Type: The franchise type identifies in general is the type of work involved in running the franchise. There are five main categories, retail franchises, management franchises, single operator manual, single operator executive and investment.

Franchising: A method of doing business within a given industry that involves at least two parties; the franchisor and the franchisee. The contract binding the two parties is the franchise.

Franchisor: The parent company or person that grants, for a fee and other considerations, the right to use its name and system of business operations.

Home-based franchises: These are franchises that can be run from home from a small office. The franchise investment is usually lower with a home-based franchise.

Initial Investment: The funds needed to initially set up a franchise and begin trading. This amount must cover the franchise fee paid to the franchisor and also includes outlay needed to secure space, purchase products, and cover any other initial set-up costs.

Investment: The franchisee invests a significant amount of money in the franchise such as a hotel. The franchisee in this case will be personally be working at arm's length from the franchise and will employ a management team to operate it.

Management Franchise: The franchisee will be using their experience to grow the business and control staff who carry out the tasks of the job. It will require premises, which are more likely to be office than a High Street outlet. The majority of the turnover from management franchises is generated from Business to Business activities rather than from retail.

Management Service Fee: A term for Royalties, usually in the form of a fixed fee or percentage.

Marketing Plan: A marketing plan should form part of your overall business plan. The purpose of the marketing plan is to define your market, i.e. identify your customers and competitors, to outline a strategy for attracting and keeping customers and to identify and anticipate change.

Master Franchisee/License: This is a franchisee who is given the right by the franchisor to develop and sell franchises under the brand name within a certain territory. Unlike area development rights, where a franchisee can open outlets themselves within a given region, a master franchise owner must only sell franchises in a particular region.

Multi-Level Marketing (MLM): A form of distributorship in which you receive commission on your own sales and on the sales of others whom you sign up as distributors. Some MLMs are considered pyramid schemes and illegal in some countries. Some are legitimate business opportunities. Any business of this nature should be investigated closely.

Multi-Unit Franchise: The franchisor awards the right to a franchisee to operate more than one unit within a defined area based on an agreed upon development schedule.

Offer: An oral or written proposal to sell a franchise to a prospective franchisee upon understood general terms and conditions.

Operating Manual: Comprehensive guidelines advising a franchisee on how to operate the franchised business. It covers all aspects of the business, and may be separated into different manuals addressing such subjects as accounting, personnel, advertising, promotion and maintenance.

Product Format Franchise: Once the rights to market a product or service have been acquired, you may offer other products along side your "product franchise." For example you may have a service station that sells a brand of gasoline, but you are not restricted on the other products or services that you can sell. Many times these are not true franchises, but can be considered distributorships.

Regional Franchise: Buys the rights from a master franchisee or the original franchisor to sell franchises in a defined region.

Renewal: The rights given to a franchisee to renew their franchise business once the initial period set out in the franchise agreement has lapsed. The franchise agreement should also state the terms and conditions under which both parties agree that the business relationship can or cannot be renewed.

Retail Franchise: The franchise will occupy retail premises, selling products or services during retail hours for 'walk-in' retail. The business is totally dependent on the premises and turnover is achieved from walk-in consumers.

Royalty Fees: Ongoing fees paid to the franchisor by franchisees in respect of ongoing training and support services provided, usually a percentage of turnover.

Single Operator Executive: (Also referred to as a 'white collar' Job Franchise) - the franchisee will be working at the franchise which usually takes the form of a trade supplying, selling and delivering products or service. It may be mobile, home-based or requiring small office premises. The type of work is executive.

Single Operator Manual (Also referred to as Job Franchise): The franchisee will be working at the franchise which usually takes the form of a trade supplying, selling and delivering products or service. It may be mobile, home-based or requiring small office premises.

Termination: Refers to the legal provisions by which either party in the relationship may terminate the contract, e.g., for breach of contract.

Territory/Area: That 'exclusive' portion of land, on a national, regional/area, county, metropolitan or postcode basis, which is allocated to franchisees as part of the franchise package.

Total Investment: The amount of money estimated for complete set up of a franchisee's business, including the initial investment, the working capital, and subsequent additions to inventory and equipment deemed necessary for a fully operational and profitable enterprise.

Turnkey Package: A package that includes all the systems, information and equipment a franchisee needs to be able to 'turn the key' and start trading.

Working Capital: A major cause of business failure is not having enough cash in the bank, trade credit, borrowing capacity or cash flow to meet start-up expenses and see the business through any unusual dips and changes in its daily activity. Initially funds are needed to pay first and last month's rent, utility deposits, licenses and any number of incidental costs. As it takes time to build up a new business the first months are usually loss months, which need to be financed.

Chapter 40: Conclusion

Franchising is growing fast. It's proven to be the safest way of starting your own business and nine out of ten franchisees; the people who run franchised businesses say they are in profit.

Franchising is not limited to burger bars; there are hundreds of businesses that are franchised in the UK, Europe and USA from plumbing through retailing to will-writing services. Whatever kind of business you want the chances are there is one to suit you.

The industry is growing too, although not as fast as many franchisors would like, 39% say a lack of suitable franchisees is thwarting growth; so they are looking for you. Two-thirds of those who go into franchising were in salaried employment immediately before taking out their current franchise.

Training is provided by 100% of franchisors, with 73% providing in-house training. Encouragingly, the relationship between franchisors and franchisees is very good, with the majority (86%) saying that their dealing with one the other was healthy.

But before you start looking for a franchise it pays to do your homework.

1. Find out about the concept.

2. Check whether franchising would suit you; running a franchise is not everyone's cup of tea.

3. Check what you can afford; you have to pay for franchises so if you want to start a business on a shoestring you may have to forget franchising.

4. Check what kind of franchises are available; there is a huge range so there may well be one to suit your own interests and needs.

5. Pick the right one for you; running a franchised business can often be hard work so you have to be fully committed to it or it risks becoming drudgery.

6. Know where to find out about franchising and get expert help.

7. Talk to several people who already have franchised businesses to find out what it's like at the sharp end.

Contact the franchisors that you are interested in; there are details on all the major franchisors and many of the smaller ones in-online franchise directory.

Let's not forget that franchising is a way of setting up in business for yourself but not on your own. With a franchise you run the business, but using methods that have been already tried and tested by another company, called the franchisor.

You pay the franchisor for a package that gives you an exclusive 'territory' and allows you to use its brand name, methods of operation, technology or products for a certain period, say five years, on a renewable contract. Once accepted as franchisee you get technical and/or business training, operation manuals, often marketing help and sometimes accounting or other administration services. In return, you agree to run the business according to the franchisor's methods and standards.

Make sure you are well briefed about what franchising means in practical terms before you start looking for a franchise. It's worth investing time and money on research; it could save you far greater sums and a lot of heartache later on.

Good Luck!!